A BLANDFORD
GARDENING HANDBOOK

# CONTAINER GARDENING

Peter McHoy

BLANDFORD PRESS
POOLE · NEW YORK · SYDNEY

First published in the UK 1986 by Blandford Press,
Link House, West Street, Poole, Dorset, BH15 1LL

Distributed in the United States by
Sterling Publishing Co., Inc.,
2 Park Avenue, New York, N.Y. 10016

Distributed in Australia by
Capricorn Link (Australia) Pty Ltd
PO Box 665, Lane Cove, NSW 2066

**British Library Cataloguing in Publication Data**

McHoy, Peter
    Container gardening.—(A Blandford gardening
handbook)
    1. Container gardening
    I. Title
    635.9'86              SB418


ISBN 0 7137 1576 6 (Hardback)
07137 1579 0 (Paperback)

All photographs by Peter McHoy
and line drawings by Paula Chasty.

Typeset by Megaron Typesetting, Bournemouth, Dorset

Printed in Portugal by Printer Portuguesa

# CONTENTS

# INTRODUCTION

An eye-catching container almost invariably brings admiration from passers-by and immense satisfaction to the grower. Sadly, really stunning window-boxes, baskets and tubs are the exception – more often they are mediocre or down-right poor.

The reason is not difficult to find. Plants in containers of all kinds need a

The smaller the garden, the more important it is to make use of all available space. Here window-boxes and hanging baskets make use of vertical space. Containers stand on the barbecue when it is not in use.

If you have a really decorative container, plant in a restrained way so that the flowers do not detract from the ornament.

great deal more attention than plants in the rest of the garden. They have all the odds stacked against them: a severely limited root-run, usually gross over-crowding by comparison with normal spacing, and a volume of soil that is likely to dry out in a depressingly short time in hot weather.

Yet despite all these handicaps, the results can be stunning. Of course, for some people with only a tiny garden (or none at all) container gardening is the only form of outdoor gardening possible.

In this book I have tried to take a prac-tical and realistic look at container gar-dening. I have examined as objectively as possible the pros and cons of the many containers, been honest about what you can expect from some of the most popu-lar plants for them, and aimed to point out both pitfalls and possibilities in growing techniques. The result should mean fewer disappointments, more suc-cesses, and the desire to 'have a go'.

# 1·USING SPACE CREATIVELY

Container gardening is not about using containers for the sake of it. Most plants do much better in the ground, and if you can plant directly into the ground instead of using a container do so. The plant will have a less restricted root-run, a better reservoir of nutrients, and of course you will have a lot less watering to worry about.

Containers can, however, bring colour and interest to parts of the garden that would otherwise be without plants, and they sometimes form an integral part of the garden design, serving as a focal point. Hanging baskets and window-boxes bring colour and interest to otherwise plantless space, and containers of other kinds are at their best enlivening otherwise potentially dull spots, such as areas of paving. Many containers are, of course, attractive in their own right, even without plants. The more attractive kinds can be used as a focal point.

Ornaments, especially containers, have played an important role in garden land-scaping for over 400 years. Nowadays, with so many types of container in so many materials, from terracotta to plastic, and including glass-fibre and recon-stituted stone, some of them expensive but most quite cheap, it is easy to be tempted into buying the containers first and worrying about where to put them afterwards. Yet buying the right container needs thought: it should complement and blend with its surrounds. This applies not only to urns and ornate centrepieces but also to window-boxes and containers for porches; they will be very conspicuous, and it is not easy to hide a mistake in taste (although there are some tricks you can try to improve the appearance of a window-box; see p. 51).

Good pots and troughs are expensive, so there is no point in paying a lot of money if you are going to hide them away: if you have invested in a distinctive container it is worth making an obvious feature of it.

Try to avoid impulse getting the better of good taste. In a tiny modern garden a classical urn on a tall pedestal is not going to look right with the rotary clothes drier and a collection of children's toys. If you are not to be accused of being ostentatious, be more modest and per-haps let the plants play a more important role than the container itself.

The larger the garden, the more op-tions you have, and the more scope for fairly ornate pieces that can form a focal point without looking pretentious. In a large garden the containers can actually play much the same role as statuary.

A group of containers is often far more effective than single ones dotted about the garden. Here a gravel base has been set into the lawn to make a more positive feature of the pots.

Glazed and decorated containers like this are expensive to buy, but are a worthwhile investment if you can create the right setting for them.

In a large garden a suitable urn can provide a focal point that forms an integral part of the design; for someone with little more than a balcony, container gardening may be the only form of gardening possible. For most gardens, however, containers are a way of punctuating the design.

## PLAIN OR ORNATE?

The showier the plant, the plainer the container can be. If plants are to trail extensively, there is little point in paying for an ornate container that you are not going to see or appreciate.

As some of the more ornate pieces really serve more as ornaments than as plant holders, and rarely fulfil both functions well, it is worth resisting the urge to cram every container with plants.

The heavier the planting, the plainer the container ought to be; the more ornate the container, the more restrained the planting − and occasionally it may be best to steel yourself not to plant it at all.

## ARRANGING POTS

Isolated containers can work effectively, but they need to be bold or interesting. The planted wheelbarrow illustrated on

9

This picture demonstrates two points: the most unlikely objects can be pressed into use as containers; and you can have an attractive display even on a site exposed to the blast of sea winds. These planted boots and other objects were spotted by the author on a quay in Devon, England.

Even a collection of plants in ordinary clay pots can take on a significance that would be completely lacking if they were dotted around in isolation.

page 78 and the converted garden table on page 79 are examples of heavily planted containers that need to be seen in isolation − other containers would detract from the impact. Usually, though, urns, tubs and vases are more effective grouped, provided that you do not try to mix too many materials. Groups of terracotta pots can be particularly effective.

## A PLANTING POLICY

In other chapters in this book there are planting suggestions for various types of container, and the list of plants in

A tall garden ornament as a centrepiece to the garden, perhaps set on a plinth, is best planted with fairly low-growing but colourful plants. Mixed lobelia has been used for the edge of this urn.

Chapter 8 has suggestions for the type of container in which they might be grown. Achieving the right combination of plants is not easy, however, and trying to cram too many different plants into the same container is a recipe for disappointment unless you know the plants well and have seen that the combination can work. Some very expert growers of hanging baskets will pack in as many as a dozen different types of plant in one basket, but for an amateur who lacks the

Simple planting with just a few subjects is often more effective than a miscellany of different plants. Here yellow Afro-French marigolds and red petunias have been used for simple but effective contrast.

Wide steps are a convenient place for pots, which also help to enhance the steps themselves.

This shallow container has almost been hidden by these mesembryanthemums — but be warned that these plants open only when it is sunny and warm, so they can be disappointing in a poor summer.

What would otherwise have been a very uninteresting spot has been brought to life here by using a variety of plants (note the couple of evergreens for winter interest too) and containers at different heights.

A wheelbarrow display like this is not easy to achieve. It demands regular attention, feeding, and dead-heading. There is little else in this tiny front garden, but it is still eye-catching.

intimate knowledge of the plants (and indeed specific varieties), this is a risky course. In tubs and pots, in particular, it is generally safer to keep to one type of plant or colour in each container, and to introduce other colours or plants in separate pots. The same also applies to some extent to troughs and window-boxes. Just a few different plants are likely to have much more impact than half a dozen or more competing with each other; instead of looking colourful they frequently look a mess.

This small garden would appear to offer little scope, but, by using containers at different heights, including some on poles, it is striking even from a distance.

A plain brick wall can be enhanced by a simple trellis on which to hang a variety of containers.

## BALCONY AND ROOF GARDENS

Although most of the pictures in this book show containers in a garden setting, container gardening is particularly relevant for anyone with a tiny garden or perhaps just a balcony or space for a couple of window-boxes. For these gardeners, container gardening may be the only form of gardening possible other than growing houseplants indoors. If you are in that situation, it is even more important to choose both containers and plants carefully.

Roof gardens offer more scope than balconies, but the problems are similar. You can follow most of the advice in this book if you have a roof garden, but lightweight containers are essential, and peat-based composts (or a mixture of peat-based and loam-based composts) should be chosen so that the weight is kept down. You should always take professional advice from a qualified structural engineer or an architect before converting your roof into a garden. The weight of containers and wet compost can be substantial.

# 2·HANGING BASKETS

Well-grown hanging baskets can be breathtakingly spectacular. Sadly, they are more often disappointing. To succeed with a hanging basket you need a good knowledge of plants (or a planting plan to guide you), some flair for arrangement, and a great deal of dedication (even forsaking your holidays if a neighbour is unable to take over for the period).

Although this chapter is about hanging baskets, the term has to be interpreted loosely. The days when the old wire 'basket' reigned supreme have long since gone. Its position has to some extent been usurped by plastic 'baskets', hanging pots, and even recycled cellulose fibre containers, not to mention hanging columns. There are, of course, half-baskets that sit snugly against the wall.

It is worth giving careful thought to the various types of container: none of them will remove the need for vigilance and constant attention, but some make better containers than others.

## FULL BASKETS

**Wire baskets** The traditional hanging basket, perhaps too easily dismissed as being 'old-fashioned'. For many professionals this is still the basket of first choice, and, if you can persevere and overcome the problems of lining it, it should produce very good results. Even galvanised wire baskets will last for many years, but most of them are now plastic-coated. Once the plants grow you should not be conscious of the wires anyway.

A few wire baskets have a flat base; the claimed advantage is that this makes them more stable and easier to plant. A round-bottomed basket should present no problems if you nestle it in a large pot or a bucket while you plant it up.

BUYING HINTS Avoid wire baskets that have a small mesh – it will drive you mad trying to plant through the sides. You can cut sections out with wire-cutters, and there is a technique for getting plants through small holes (see page 30), but there is no point in buying yourself a problem. Baskets with a mesh less than about 4 cm (1½ in) are best avoided.

The bigger the basket the bolder and better the display should be, but you have to weigh this (literally) against the drawbacks of handling and supporting a very heavy basket. The spectacular 36 cm (14 in) and larger baskets that you see decorating the streets in some more plant-conscious towns will probably

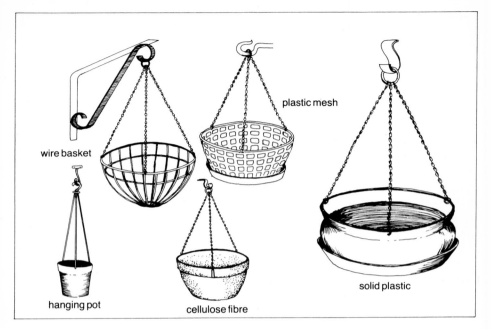

wire basket

plastic mesh

hanging pot

cellulose fibre

solid plastic

be hanging from lamp standards which are hardly likely to buckle under the weight. It is different if you are expecting most of the small brackets sold for hanging baskets to do the same job: even if the bracket itself is strong, you have to be sure that it is securely fixed. A large basket with wet loam-based compost can exert a considerable strain on bracket and fixings.

Unless you have a really good means of support, it is best to go for a 30 cm (12 in) basket. This will be quite heavy enough to keep lifting for turning and other attention.

You may not have much choice, but where you have the option choose the deepest basket that you can find. This

Some basket types.

will provide a better volume of compost and reservoir of nutrients.

**Plastic mesh baskets** Most plastic hanging containers are solid (with drainage holes in the base), but there are also plastic 'mesh' baskets on the lines of the traditional wire basket. The mesh is generally larger of course, and the sections thicker. If well planted the slightly off-putting appearance should be hidden, but other than price there is nothing to be said for them as improvements over the wire type, which are less obtrusive while the plants are growing.

17

Try using a bucket to support the basket while you plant it. You can also stand a filled basket on a bucket if you have to take it down for any reason.

Plant the lower tiers of a basket as you proceed. Keep the root-ball intact if possible. This plant is *Cerastium tomentosum,* normally thought of as a vigorous rock plant, but useful as a hanging basket trailer too.

BUYING HINTS You are unlikely to have problems getting the plants through the holes, but you may find that moss is more difficult to keep in position with the large mesh and some of the liners sold for them are not particularly attractive (see liners, page 25).

**Solid plastic 'baskets'** These can hardly be called baskets; they are really plastic containers on a hanger. A few are quite ornate in themselves, but if your 'baskets' are to be full of cascading plants you will not see much of the actual container, so do not be too influenced by this. With rare exceptions, you will not have the opportunity to plant around the sides and base, so careful choice of plants

is even more crucial if they are to compete with an open mesh basket. They are less demanding to water as generally they do not dry out so quickly.

A few are claimed to be self-watering, but you may find that this means no more than that there is a small reservoir to collect excess water. This may help to keep the basket moist for a little longer, but do not expect too much from them as you will still have to water frequently.

A few baskets come in two pieces so that you can plant around the sides as well. The bottom half is filled with compost, the plants placed in the notches provided, then the top half clipped on before filling with compost and planting the

Carefully thread the foliage through the hole from the inside, so that the root-ball is not damaged. This is much easier if the mesh is wide.

It is worth covering the *top* of the basket with moss too. This will make it look more finished, help to conserve moisture, and reduce the likelihood of water just running off when you water.

top. These are not generally available to amateurs at the time of writing, but are quite widely used in the trade. The idea seems good, but remember that a well-grown basket without side planting holes can be more successful than one with side planting that is neglected.

BUYING HINTS Most of these baskets are made from polypropylene and should certainly last for several seasons with care; but they are not as robust as wire, and will crack or smash if the support fails and they drop from a height. Strength apart, go for one that has a good capacity: the more room there is for the root-balls and compost the better.

Aesthetic considerations cannot be ignored. There are certainly going to be a couple of months when the container is very visible, and if you are not very successful it will still be seen by the end of the season. It is a matter of personal taste whether you find white plastic more acceptable than green. Brown is perhaps the least obtrusive colour.

The hanger needs to be strong, and it should look respectable too. Some are crude to say the least, little more than something resembling a wire coat-hanger. If the 'basket' is to be a showpiece you want a hanger that does not look cheap or tatty; it will take time for the plants to hide it completely. Most plastic hangers incorporate a drip tray,

This is a reconstituted polyurethane foam liner. Whatever kind of liner you use, always place a generous amount of good compost in the bottom of the basket before planting.

If using a liner like this, you will have to arrange the side planting to correspond with the slits

which is a plus point as a dripping basket is a nuisance.

**Hanging pots** These are intended primarily for houseplants that have a cascading habit, but of course they can be used outdoors too.

Even in their larger sizes, they are primarily one-plant pots (or in the case of some trailers, several planted around the edge). They are no substitute for a proper hanging basket, but they are useful for hanging certain plants around the patio. Being suitable for indoors too you can use them for plants that are not hardy and have to be taken indoors for the winter. Be warned though that keeping any indoor hanging basket healthy through the winter is not easy. Hanging them up high usually reduces the amount

When you reach the top, position the central plant first, then fill in round the sides.

Few plastic baskets enable you to plant around the sides. This one does — the top half simply clips over the bottom after you have positioned the plants.

With the top half clipped on and more compost added, the top can be planted.

of light they receive and the plants become drawn and leggy; it is a simple matter to remove the hanger, so if possible stand the containers on a window-ledge where they will receive plenty of light.

BUYING HINTS Hanging pots are now used widely by professional growers. There is the inevitable problem of choosing which colour plastic is the least objectionable; you are likely to be faced with white, green, or brown. The latter has a lot to commend it, but the choice is yours.

**Collapsible baskets** These come in one, two or possibly three tiers. The principle is the same as that of a folding chip basket: they expand when lifted.

The picture that may come with the tiered baskets (which become larger as you progress downwards) looks full of promise, but these are not for the faint-hearted. Based on those available at the time of writing, the weight of compost, water and plants in *three* baskets is likely to be just too much for the chains and hanger, even if you can find a bracket to support the weight. If you have ever had the job of picking up a fallen basket, imagine that three times over, only worse; because as the basket above falls on the one beneath it does a magnificent job of producing squashed plants. By the time it has collapsed several times you will probably give up.

Petunias and lobelias can both be tricky plants for hanging baskets if you are inclined to let them dry out occasionally. If never allowed to go short of water, though, they can be very effective. *Thunbergia alata* has also been used to climb up the supporting chains.

A well-grown basket should be a ball of colour, with little or no container showing.

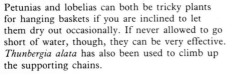

A typical mixed planting basket – effective but often difficult to keep looking good as the various plants may have different growth rates and flowering periods.

Having condemned these baskets, it is only fair to say that one of the most magnificent baskets that I have seen was just such a tier of three, which had become a column of colour with no sign of the baskets beneath; but all the joints and supporting hook had been reinforced by the grower after earlier collapses. So have a go, but make sure that you have a *very* strong support, and reinforce the joints and hanger. The ones you are likely to find now, however, have one or two tiers, and these should cause no problem.

BUYING HINTS Try a two-tier! There is not much point in buying a single basket of this type because a traditional wire basket will be stronger and easier to plant (trying to get plants through the tiny mesh will drive you to despair).

**Cellulose fibre hanging pots** These sound unpromising and they hardly look elegant. Peat-coloured and rather

Trailing lobelia remains one of the most popular basket plants, despite its short life if the basket dries out. Looked after, it can be really impressive.

chunky-looking, you cannot really expect to get more than a couple of seasons out of them, though you can be fairly certain of a second year's use.

They are actually very successful, perhaps because they hold a good volume

One of the most difficult things to achieve in a hanging basket is good downward growth. Few trailers really cascade very much in a basket. Nasturtiums will, as this picture shows, but you need to choose a suitable variety and be prepared to keep the plant trimmed if necessary, and spraying to control blackfly will almost certainly be necessary.

of compost and do not dry out as rapidly as a wire basket.

You can cut holes in the sides with a sharp craft knife if you want to put some plants in the sides. Whether this is necessary depends on how well you can grow your plants; if you feed and water as often as you should you can expect suitable plants to cascade over and hide the container anyway, but if you have

doubts about your ability to achieve this sort of display it may be worth cutting out a few triangular holes and planting around the sides.

BUYING HINTS These are worth trying. Even though you will have to replace after a few years, there is no moss or liner to buy and you may find the little extra cost over the years is worth it if the results are better (it really depends how well you can grow a traditional basket).

## HALF BASKETS

Most gardeners think first of full baskets. There is perhaps a sneaking feeling that a half basket is somehow second-best, not quite a 'real' hanging basket.

If you hang your basket in an open position, away from a wall, a full basket is undoubtedly a more spectacular sight. Most home baskets are supported on wall brackets, however, which really means that the basket becomes one-sided anyway unless you are prepared to turn it twice a week to keep it symmetrical. The dedicated and the energetic may well want to embark on this course, but for those without the time, inclination or effort to manhandle the heavy baskets twice a week it is an unrealistic proposition (though a swivel-hook like the one illustrated will make turning relatively easy). If you are not going to turn the basket, a half basket could be just as attractive.

Of course there are variations on the commercial half baskets; if you are fortunate enough to own an old manger, this will make a magnificent container.

## LINERS

**Sphagnum moss,** the traditional basket liner, is still hard to better. Most garden

Red and blue lobelia together with mixed petunias and *Thunbergia alata* go to make this basket, which is made from cellulose fibre. Although planted in the top alone, the container is already being covered.

Petunias make superb container plants on their own, but keep them well watered and be prepared to dead-head and feed regularly to get a display like this.

centres sell bags of moss during the planting season, and your local florist may also be able to help. You must, however, be generous and use a thick layer; and ideally cover the surface of the compost too once planting is finished.

If you water frequently and thoroughly, the moss should continue to live, at least for most of the summer, and remain green and attractive. Frequently, however, it dries out and takes on a pale, washed-out appearance; fortunately by that time the plants should have begun to fill out and hide the moss anyway.

**Polythene (polyethylene)** is frequently used because it is cheap and readily available (you can always use an old plastic bag). Black polythene is usually preferred to transparent, but it does not seem to make much difference to the plants and both clear and black can look unattractive.

It is not easy to line a basket with polythene; you always seem to end up with crinkles that are impossible to smooth, and it never seems to shape well to the contours of the basket. You can manage, of course, by slitting the polythene and overlapping it where necessary. If you are planting in the sides, simply pierce holes wherever they are needed.

**Coir fibre liners** are something of a rarity, but you may find them in garden centres. If you have not encountered these, they are made from jute and coconut fibre, and look rather like a coconut on one side and sacking on the other. Slits ensure a reasonable fit in the basket, and although you can side-plant through the slits this is not easy. The coconut fibre side faces out; the hessian side should be in contact with the compost. These liners have little to offer in comparison with moss, although they will last longer.

**Foam plastic liners** are more widely available, and are easy to use. Choose the size that is closest to your basket. Because the material is very soft and malleable it is quite easy to side-plant through the

Half baskets or wall baskets are often a better solution than trying to hang a traditional basket too close to a wall.

A basket in a tree. Although not an ideal position, it is another way to add interest in a small garden.

This basket contains four of the most traditional basket plants: trailing lobelia, petunias, geraniums and fuchsias.

slits. These liners should last a couple of seasons before they begin to disintegrate.

**Rigid plastic liners** are not everyone's idea of a good liner. They are usually sold to go with a particular type of plastic mesh basket. If you are going to line this kind of basket with a solid liner, it may be better to buy a solid container to start with.

**Compressed peat liners** are intended to fit into plastic-covered wire mesh baskets of the right size, so it is best to use them in the same manufacturer's basket to be sure of a good fit.

You might be forgiven for wondering why you should buy a wire basket in the first place if you are going to use a solid liner. You could try cutting holes in the liner, but a solid plastic 'basket' is likely to be a better choice if you do not want to plant in the sides.

## WHERE TO HANG THEM

It is much easier to describe the ideal site for a hanging basket than to find it. A sunny aspect is likely to suit the majority of basket plants, but of course the sunnier and hotter it is the more watering and care the baskets will need. Winds can devastate a basket, so avoid any wind-tunnels such as you often find between buildings, and very exposed sites. The corner of a house can be particularly windy.

It is tempting to have a basket beneath a porch, but this is seldom successful because the plants will be drawn towards the light and unless you turn the basket frequently it will become very unattractive on the 'dark' side. This is a position where a swivel hook can be particularly worthwhile, then you can easily turn the basket a quarter of a turn each day.

The ideal position for a full basket is one that receives light from all sides. In reality most are supported on wall brackets. You could hang them from a patio overhead or pergola.

Baskets are sometimes hung in deciduous trees that do not have a very heavy canopy (an apple tree should be all right if you want to try this), but they seldom thrive in the shade and though they look pretty it is best to have several baskets that you rotate regularly if you want to make a feature of tree baskets. You will, of course, have to find a low branch of suitable thickness.

**Brackets** need to be strong, and they should be large enough to hold the basket clear from the wall, *when it has been planted;* otherwise the plants on the wall side will be damaged. It is also worth checking the *width* of the bracket at the point where the hook goes; some broad ones look decorative but are too wide for many hooks.

Some brackets look very ornate, but never overlook the practical considerations. If you already have the basket, make sure the hook will slip over the lip — some made from a broad piece of metal may be too wide for some basket hooks. Strength is especially important if you have a large basket.

Swivel hooks are useful for fixing to a beam. They enable you to turn the basket without having to take it down.

A hanging column is also shown here. You can sometimes buy these, or you could try making one yourself.

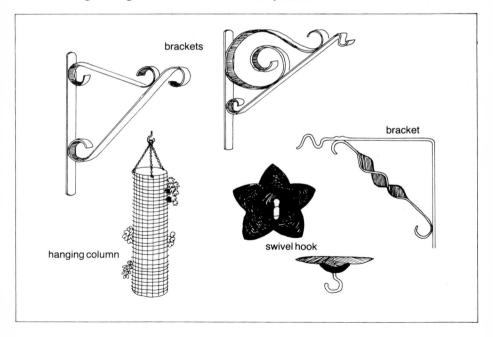

brackets

bracket

hanging column

swivel hook

## PLANTING A MOSS-LINED WIRE BASKET

1) Balance the basket on a bucket or small bowl for stability. A few types of wire basket have a flat base, which you can stand on a flat surface, but the majority have a round base and need supporting. Have everything to hand: plants, compost and liner.

2) Place a thick layer of moss in the base; aim for at least 2.5 cm (1 in), as it will compress anyway with the weight of compost. Bring the moss up to the level of the first row of plants, and add compost (see page 88) to the same level.

3) Insert the plants from the inside, rather than trying to push the root-ball through the mesh. As most plants used for the sides are likely to be small seedlings, such as lobelia, the root-balls should not be so large that you have to remove any compost from the roots.

4) You should have little difficulty if the mesh is large, but with small-mesh baskets the prospect of getting the leaves through can seem an impossible task, especially for plants with thickish, brittle leaves such as *Begonia semperflorens*. There is a trick of the trade, however, that works like magic for most plants.

Take a piece of polythene (perhaps cut from an old bag) or a piece of thick paper about 8 × 10 cm (3 × 4 in), and roll the

A hanging basket in the classic style – lobelia and alyssum, French marigolds, and petunias, together with a small-leaved ivy.

30

leaves in this, rather as if you were rolling a cigarette. Even plants with brittle leaves can usually be handled safely if you do it carefully. You will end up with a cigar-like roll that you can then push through the mesh. Once the end is through, pull it from the outside too, then when the whole roll is through the wrapper can be unfurled and the plant is safely through a seemingly impossibly small hole.

5) Add more moss to the height of the next layer, making sure it is well packed around the plants just inserted. Pile compost behind the moss, but leave a cavity in the centre as you approach the top of the basket, to allow for the roots of the plants to be inserted in the top of the basket.

6) You will probably be using some larger plants in the top of the basket, and pot-grown geraniums (pelargoniums) and fuchsias for instance may have a large root-ball that will have to be reduced if you are to fit them in. Start by removing an inch or so from the bottom, teasing the roots out carefully and spreading them out as you plant. Do not remove more compost than absolutely necessary. It will almost certainly be more

A plastic basket containing standard lobelia (not trailing), fibrous-rooted begonias, petunias, verbena, and a geranium.

The basket shown being planted on page 20.

Do not overlook the possibility of using greenhouse or house plants for a basket in a light position in a porch. This basket contains *Plectranthus australis, P. coleoides marginatus,* and *Setcreasea purpurea.*

convenient to plant the large central plant first, then fill in the sides. Trailing plants, such as cascading fuchsias and ivy-leaved geraniums, can be given a start by planting them at a slight angle over the side.

7) A moss basket will look more finished if you also cover the top of the compost with a thick layer of moss. You will not see it once the basket is in position of course, but some of the best baskets I have seen have been covered with moss at the top, and it may be that it maintains additional humidity for the plants and

helps to keep the compost moist for longer. You can still put a layer of moss over the top of other types of baskets of course.

## USING A FOAM LINER

Make sure the liner is a good fit for the basket (it may be necessary to overlap the liner at the slits). Arrange the plants in

Alyssum, French marigolds, geraniums, and small-leaved ivies.

Fuchsias are often seen to best effect if planted alone – in a mixed basket the flowers often become lost among the other plants.

the side of the basket to coincide with the slits in the liner.

### PLANTING A SOLID PLASTIC BASKET

Most solid plastic baskets can be planted only in the top, but one type comes in two halves, enabling some plants to be inserted in the sides.

### PUTTING THEM OUT

Resist the temptation to put your basket out straight away; if at all possible give it ten days to two weeks in a greenhouse, or failing that a cold frame (you can stand it on a bucket or small bowl). This will help the plants to become established and they will be that much more advanced by the time you come to hang the basket outside. Of course if the greenhouse is kept very warm you will need to harden the plants off again by keeping the basket in a frame for a week, or at least take it in at night.

If you have no choice but to put it straight outside, it is worth keeping it in a warm sheltered place for a couple of weeks, taking it in at night. This means keeping it supported on a bucket or something similar, but putting the basket out in an exposed place too quickly is one cause of failure.

Before you put the basket outside, spray with a suitable insecticide (check on the label to make sure the basket does not contain plants that may be damaged by the spray). Starting with a clean,

The appearance of the basket and liner should not be a problem once the plants have grown, but it is important to choose plants that will trail and give good cover if you want this effect.

healthy basket can make a big difference to the long-term prospects. If there are any signs of fungus diseases (such as rots or leaf spots) use a fungicide too; though diseases should not be a problem at this stage. On the other hand, pests such as aphids will always welcome a meal of fresh young plants.

*Calceolaria* 'Sunshine', good in a mixed basket as well as on its own.

Ivy-leaved geraniums – the pale wall behind and the lack of conflicting plants in the basket makes the most of a simple planting.

Petunias and red salvias have been used in the top of this basket; mixed lobelia has been used for the bottom.

## *PLANTING SCHEMES*

No matter how carefully you plant a basket, nor how well you care for it afterwards, it will never rise above the ordinary unless you have the right plants in it. It is relatively easy to decide how *many* plants you can fit in; to some extent you will be restricted by how many rootballs can be accommodated. Some baskets made up by professionals contain a very large number of plants, perhaps as many as 20, but equally effective baskets can be achieved with perhaps half a dozen plants, or even less. Much depends on the type and size of the plants.

For some reason most hanging baskets seem to contain as many different plants as it is possible to cram in, perhaps in the hope of plenty of colour. The result can look a mess, one plant hiding another, and all growing into each other in a way that looks a jumble. If you must have lots of different plants, at least try to make the baskets symmetrical, repeating the plant in one side in the other.

Rather than look for lots of different colours and types of plants, concentrate on a good combination of habits: trailers, cascaders (those that tend to arch out over the top), compact but bushy plants, and perhaps a majestic upright-grower (maybe a good geranium or an upright fuchsia) for the centrepiece. This way you should have plenty of colour and interest without the plants competing with each other too much.

Coleus may seem an unlikely candidate for a hanging basket, and it certainly is not a good choice for a very windy or exposed position. In the right place, however, the result can be impressive. It is important to choose a variety suitable for baskets, such as this one which is 'Poncho'.

Although not so popular with amateurs, some really fine baskets can be achieved with single-subject planting. This is perhaps more popular for greenhouse hanging baskets but works well outdoors too. You need to select the plants carefully of course, but impatiens, *Calceolaria* 'Sunshine', and even petunias can be very effective. If you want to be more adventurous you could try a basket of sanvitalia (this needs a warm, sunny spot) and even coleus can look very striking. Take care with the coleus, however, as they need a sheltered position; you also need to choose a special semi-trailing basket variety such as 'Poncho'.

Some planting ideas are shown in the accompanying pictures, but be prepared to modify these to suit your own taste, and the plants available. Nasturtiums can make an impressive basket plant, but you will probably have constant problems with blackfly, and many people dislike their smell, so substitute something else if you do not like the idea of nasturtiums in a particular plan.

You may also have problems finding a particular variety, and often an alternative will be equally good. Sometimes, however, you will have to be careful to find a substitute with the right habit; some impatiens, for example, are far too lank and tall in comparison with the more compact varieties suitable for baskets. Chapter 8 gives suggestions where it is particularly important to check that you select a suitable variety.

# 3·WINDOW-BOXES

The difference between window-boxes and troughs can be a matter of perhaps 1.2 m (4 ft), for many of the containers sold as troughs can also be used as window-boxes. It all depends where you put them. Frequently, however, the sheer size or weight of some of the troughs means that unless you have a very substantial window-sill these have to be regarded as troughs. If you can support them safely, however, they usually make very good window-boxes because of their capacity.

## THE QUESTION OF SIZE

Size is extremely important. You need a box that is large enough to hold a reasonable reservoir of soil to support the plants easily, and big enough to take a reasonable selection of plants.

A depth of 15 cm (6 in) is really the minimum you should consider, and even 20 cm (8 in) is only just adequate. Bear in mind that you have to deduct space for a layer of drainage material and say 2.5 cm (1 in) between the compost and the top of the box to make watering easier.

Length does not matter so much, apart from ease of handling. A 1.8 m (6 ft) window-sill might be better with two 90 cm (3 ft) boxes, and a 1.2 m (4 ft) space better filled with two 60 cm (2 ft) boxes, if only to make the job of manhandling them that much easier. A large box is heavy and awkward to lift to a height. If you do use several smaller boxes instead of one large one, it is best to use a false front (see page 51) so that the display looks as though it is one continuous box.

The width (from front to back) will make a substantial difference to the type of display that you can achieve. A box with a width of only 15 cm (6 in) will not offer as much scope as one 20 cm (8 in) wide, which will probably give you the chance to squeeze in another row of plants, or to use bigger growers. If you want to keep the plants in pots (perhaps to make it easier to change the display), extra width will make a big difference.

If you make your own boxes (there are instructions for making one on page 46), you can make the box to fit the space (bear in mind that you will need a few inches either side of a recessed window to manoeuvre the box), but there is no real problem if you have to buy a box and are unable to find one the right size. Simply hang the box just below the window using special brackets; then it will not matter if the box is a little wider than the actual window.

This steel and ceramic trough is being planted with individual pot-grown plants – generally preferable to box-grown plants.

The plant being firmed is a verbena. The other plants are *Calceolaria* 'Sunshine', *Cineraria maritima*, and *Chrysanthemum paludosum* (mini-marguerite). The colour of this window-box or trough can be changed by sliding in ceramic tiles of your choice.

## MATERIALS

As some materials are likely to cost you perhaps seven times more than others, you may be guided to some extent by price as much as design and quality. If your window-box is to be a key feature, it is worth thinking about some of the more expensive but attractive and long-lasting boxes. Much depends on how you intend to use the boxes: if you are planting lots of trailing plants, or perhaps hostas with large leaves that will hide most of the container during the summer, there is no point in going for an elaborate design. On the other hand, if you intend to grow mainly dwarf evergreen shrubs, which will probably have an upright habit, the container will be very visible and will either enhance the display or detract from it.

If you plan to use a false front, then of course there is no point in choosing expensive and highly decorative window-boxes. The plainer and more functional the container the better. Plastics predominate, but there are lots of other materials too, ranging from steel to recycled cellulose fibre.

**Asbestos-cement** With the many apprehensions about the dangers of asbestos, you may be reluctant to introduce it into your garden, and the appearance is very austere. Asbestos-cement is also a very heavy material, and you will not want to move a filled box around the garden. Despite all these drawbacks this type of container is well worth considering for say a permanent planting of dwarf shrubs and conifers, where the generous size is better for the plants and allows a better arrangement.

The pre-pasted wallpaper trough shown being planted on pages 52–3.

POTENTIAL Perhaps best used as troughs or for a permanent planting of dwarf shrubs, where good proportions are particularly useful.

*If you are worried about the asbestos* it is important to keep the problem in perspective. If a few fibres do come loose in the garden they are not likely to do much harm, but you should avoid drilling extra drainage holes in this material. The fibres will also be less likely to come loose if you paint the box (emulsion paint will do). Some are already painted when you buy them (a smooth white finish suggests that it has been painted). Painted or unpainted, they are not particularly elegant.

**Ceramic and steel** If you have not seen one of these window-boxes they are probably hard to visualise. Only one make is known to me, and this is not widely available. They should, however, appeal to the artistically sensitive as you can have as many different finishes as there are ceramic tiles in the shops. The steel framework is actually unobtrusive, and this holds the ceramic tiles that slide into slots in the frame. The frame comes in various finishes, but black looks particularly good, and you buy the tiles to suit your taste. There are no proper

This box has a permanent planting of hebe in the background, ivy in the front, with *Campanula carpatica* in the middle − which can be replaced with other seasonal plants when it has finished flowering.

drainage holes, though some excess moisture would seep out through the joints. You may therefore prefer to use an inner plastic box, although you will have to find one of suitable dimensions.

POTENTIAL  Bright and gay, or subtle if you prefer, but a window-box that will give you lots of scope to express your individual tastes.

You can also buy 'window bars' that slot into the box and are secured into the structure of the building. There are probably better ways of making your home secure, however, and prison-like bars are not everyone's idea of enhancing a window-box.

**Glass-reinforced cement**  As window-boxes their use must be limited because of their weight and large size, which are likely to be too substantial for a window-sill in a typical home. However, the dimensions are usually ideal for the plants, especially if you want to grow dwarf shrubs in them, and it is well worth considering them as troughs even if they are not a practical proposition for your window-sill.

Traditional window-box plants – geraniums, petunias and trailing lobelia. It is easy to see why they are so popular.

Some people are put off them because they are mistaken for asbestos-cement, but they contain no asbestos. The cement is used to bind glass fibres, which produce high strength despite thin walls.

POTENTIAL  Well worth considering if you have a suitable sill and can manage to cope with the weight (which is substantial even when empty). There are various tasteful designs and finishes.

**Glass-reinforced plastic (GRP)**  You may know this material as glass-fibre. It is an expensive material but some manufacturers will produce it in special colours to match your requirements (hardly necessary unless you are very particular), and other containers are available as very realistic-looking imitation lead. They are light, and the larger sizes should have a reinforcing bar for rigidity. Generally they are made to generous proportions with a good depth and width. You can also expect a long, maintenance-free life from them.

POTENTIAL  If you can afford the cost, some of the more elaborate GRP window-boxes will actually enhance your home if the setting is right, and the generous dimensions will suit the plants. The problem may be finding a window-sill of the right proportions, as it may be difficult to find suitable brackets to hang these below the window.

**Plastic** sounds an unattractive choice, but there are plenty of designs from which to choose, and the cost is very competitive. Polypropylene is the plastic usually used, and it is generally tough and not easily degraded by sunlight. Rigid polystyrene is also used, but I have found some of these to be very short-lived, becoming brittle and easily broken if you try to lift a planted box.

Most plastic boxes will buckle or bow if you try to move them full, but this should not be a problem if you keep to reasonably small sizes. Many plastic window-boxes need to have drainage holes pierced before use. There are usually areas where the plastic is thinner so that you can easily pierce holes: make sure that you do it.

Some plastic window-boxes are reasonably generous in size, and can look quite attractive, but there is the old problem of colours. A newly-planted plastic window-box is not particularly attractive. Whites can look glaring when brand new, dirty in a very short time; greens sound as

A really bold display of cascade geraniums. If you have a plant with a bold colour it often pays to use a mass planting for real impact.

though they should be suitable for a garden setting, but somehow jar. Browns are usually a safe bet.

POTENTIAL Plastic boxes have the advantage of being relatively inexpensive (though not always so) and they are light and widely available. There is no getting away from the fact, however, that most of them lack the visual appeal of most other materials, so they are most useful where you can disguise them in some way. Do not expect them to last for ever: some might last little more than a year or two, and in the long term it may be worth

investing in more durable and attractive materials.

If you want a short-term box as an 'inner', think about something very cheap; see 'Cheap Liner Boxes' on page 52.

**Steel** is a most unlikely material for a window-box, and you are not very likely to come across one. At least one type exists, however, in a white enamelled finish. It is too shallow to be a lot of use except for small, low-growing plants. You also have to drill your own drainage holes, which is another drawback.

POTENTIAL Although it actually looks better than it sounds, is relatively inexpensive, and should have a long life, its

A home-made wooden window-box containing dwarf conifers, ivy, and *Euonymus fortunei* 'Emerald Gaiety'.

dimensions are too much of a drawback for it to be very useful.

**Recycled cellulose fibre** Clearly not a long-term solution, but they are cheap and should last for a second season. The materials looks rather like compressed peat, and is visually quite acceptable once the plants are in full bloom. They are described as patio planters, but you could use them as a trough or as a window-box.

POTENTIAL If you find that you have space for an extra window-box, and want something inexpensive, this type of planter is well worth considering. You will have no choice of size or pattern, however.

**Terracotta** Although some manufacturers describe these as window-boxes, it is perhaps debatable whether they should be regarded as troughs instead. They are heavy to use as a window-box, and you would need a very firm ledge big enough to take it securely; they are not suitable for fixing to the wall with just a couple of brackets! Some are fairly modest in price, though by no means cheap, whereas the more decorative ones are very expensive. The necessary thickness of the walls may mean that there is not very much space for compost.

POTENTIAL If you have just the right setting for this traditional material, and somewhere suitable to support the weight, it may be worth putting up with the drawbacks. Although they have

*Hebe franciscana* 'Variegata' in a plastic window-box with a false log front.

severe limitations as window-boxes, they have a much wider use as troughs.

**Timber boxes** look superb with the right plants and in a suitable setting, but they are among the most expensive to buy and are not particularly cheap to make yourself. Although the timber will rot in time, you can expect many years of use if the timber is treated with a preservative (make sure it is not toxic for plants) and supported off the sill on blocks or something similar so that the base does not sit in water.

You can also keep the box drier by keeping the soil out of contact with the sides. Possibly you could find an inner plastic box of suitable size, though you will not want to increase the cost too much. Failing that, line the box with polythene, making drainage holes in the bottom of course. Kitchen foil is another possibility.

POTENTIAL Timber can be attractive

visually, will last for many years with care, but needs regular maintenance.

## MAKING A WINDOW-BOX

Although plastic window-boxes are cheap and instant, you may feel that you want to make your own timber boxes, perhaps to fit an exact space, or because you want something that can be painted to match the house.

Home handymen will no doubt be able to produce an elegant dovetailed piece of carpentry, but the window-box described below is intended for someone without special woodworking skills or tools.

Use good quality 25 mm (1 in) deal, and cut the timber to the sizes indicated in the drawing. Simple glued and screwed joints have been used with 25×25 mm (1×1 in) battens at each corner to provide additional strength. Screw through these battens into the sides and ends. Use galvanised or zinc-plated screws and also glue the batten into position.

This one basic box can be finished in a variety of ways. If varnishing, rub smooth with glass-paper before using an exterior grade varnish, making sure it penetrates the end grain. Apply a second coat. If painting, smooth with glass-paper

Clever use of vertical space in a very tiny town garden. Low walls take the planting up to the window, where the display is continued in the boxes. You could not really have retaining walls against a normal brick-built house because of bridging the damp-proof course.

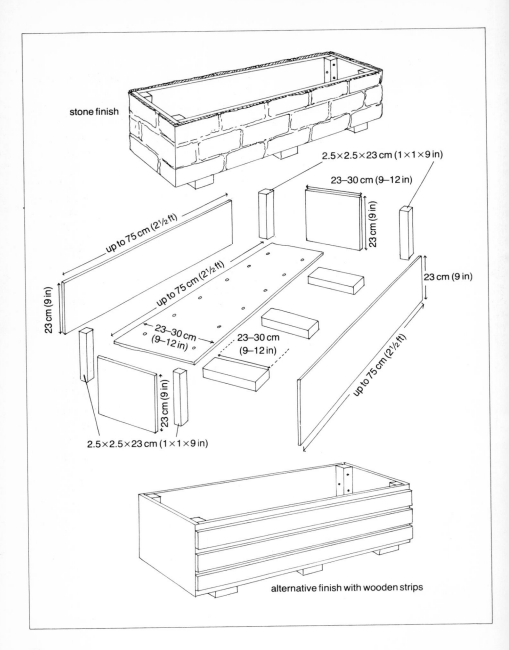

stone finish

2.5×2.5×23 cm (1×1×9 in)

23–30 cm (9–12 in)

23 cm (9 in)

up to 75 cm (2½ ft)

up to 75 cm (2½ ft)

23 cm (9 in)

23 cm (9 in)

23–30 cm (9–12 in)

23–30 cm (9–12 in)

up to 75 cm (2½ ft)

23 cm (9 in)

2.5×2.5×23 cm (1×1×9 in)

alternative finish with wooden strips

Some plastic window-boxes have a surprisingly short life and timber can be long-lasting if treated properly. Timber window-boxes are expensive to buy, but you can try making your own. This gives you the chance to make the box to fit an exact space, but avoid making it too long otherwise it will be difficult to handle.

Use good quality deal, glue and screw the pieces together, and either varnish (two coats of exterior grade) or paint (two coats of primer, two undercoats, and an enamel paint to finish).

first, apply a primer, then two layers of undercoat. Rub down when dry, then apply an enamel paint to the outside and two coats of gloss paint to the inside. Instead of painting, the front could be finished with cork bark or even small stone facing tiles glued on with a suitable adhesive. If the wood is not being

painted, treat it with a wood preservative that is harmless to plants.

## SECURING THE BOX

Securing the box properly is important at any time, but assumes even greater significance if you live in a flat or otherwise want to have a window-box above ground-floor level. Older properties may have sills large enough to take the box securely, but you should still

Never try to make do with ordinary shelf brackets, window-box brackets must be strong and specially designed for the job, with a lip to prevent the box slipping off.

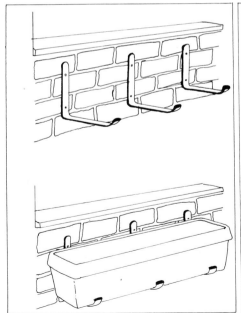

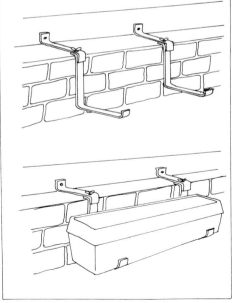

Some of the author's window-boxes ready to be taken to a show.

anchor it, perhaps by fixing eye hooks into the window-frame and passing 1 mm galvanised wire between these, through the actual box itself, by drilling a small hole through each end of the box. If you have a plastic or metal window-frame you have to find an alternative way of fixing your eye-hooks, but it should be possible to drill and plug the wall to take them.

If the sill is not flat (it may slope away from the window, to shed water more easily), cut small wedges from scrap timber to make the box horizontal. If you are using a timber box, it is worth cutting small supports for the box anyway, even if the sill is level, so that there is a circulation of air beneath the wood.

Do not overlook the possibility of fixing the window-box *below* the window. This may be essential in modern homes with only narrow sills, but is good sense anyway where there are casement windows (which open outwards), otherwise it can be difficult to open them once the plants have grown. You will also be seeing only the plants and not the back of the box too. Ordinary shelf brackets are not likely to be adequate. Not only must they be strong, but also hold the box securely with a lip that prevents the box sliding off the bracket.

A glass-reinforced cement trough – heavy but ideal for shrubs because of the large compost capacity.

Some manufacturers provide these (as a separate item at an extra cost). They naturally fit their own boxes, but may also be suitable for other makes of box as well. One make of bracket is particularly adaptable; by using various combinations of fittings supplied they can be made to fix to a whole range of windows, and can even be used to fix the box to railings.

## DISGUISING THE BOX

Some boxes are far from attractive. You may want to do something to improve appearances. False fronts are useful for this, and also where you have used two smaller boxes instead of one large one. By making it the exact width of the window recess, a false front can look particularly neat, and by using bushy plants at each end it will look as though the boxes fill the full space too.

A simple front can be made from 6 mm (¼ in) marine grade plywood, which is the height of the box and width of the window, and fixing this either to the frame of the window or to the front of the actual boxes with hooks or something similar (the exact mechanism must depend on the boxes). The plywood will need to have the ends sealed and the whole surface should be varnished or painted. You could paint these fronts to match the colour of paint used for the

A plastic window-box with lobelia, fuchsias, petunias and geraniums.

house itself, or perhaps a bright and cheerful red.

If you want something more rustic, it should also be possible to fix pieces of cork to the front of the boxes (try a florist, or failing that an aquarium shop if you have difficulty obtaining large pieces of cork bark).

## CHEAP LINER BOXES

One of the cheapest window-boxes can be found in decorating shops. These are the thin plastic troughs used for soaking ready-pasted wallpaper; they are very cheap and will actually last outside for several seasons if not handled too much.

They are not very attractive to look at, of course, but if you are using a false front this should not matter. They are also worth considering where you want an inner 'liner' for a more attractive outer box. It is worth considering these as 'liner boxes' not only where you want to protect the outer window-box but also when you want to grow on replacement displays that can be exchanged once the main display has finished. In other words you could operate an effective successional display of bloom if you have somewhere to stand the spare troughs.

A trough for pre-pasted wallpaper can be used as a cheap window-box. Plastic types will probably last for several seasons. Make sure the container has drainage holes, and place a layer of crocks (broken pots) or gravel at the bottom for good drainage. Use a potting compost, not garden soil, if you want good results.

Expanded polystyrene troughs are also available, which make cheap liner boxes, but these are very fragile and need handling with considerable care. They are unlikely to last more than a season.

## PLANTING

Planting a window-box is nowhere near as easy as it seems. At least choosing the right plant combinations is not easy; the planting is straightforward (see instructions below). Single-subject plantings do not work quite as well as they do with hanging baskets, although

Remove the plants from their pots with as little disturbance as possible. Make sure the pots have been watered an hour or so beforehand.

the illustrations on pages 43 and 45 show that they can work. Too many subjects will almost certainly lack impact: the plants will fight with each other for room and attention, and the result will not be very striking.

There is a great deal of scope for individual planting designs, but a few are suggested on pages 58 to 60 if you need a starting point. In most cases alternative varieties will do just as well, but sometimes you need to choose alternatives with a similar compact habit: you will find a reference to this point in Chapter 8 where you need to be particularly careful.

Although individual planting schemes are important, it is worth looking at window-boxes in a wider context before coming down to individual plants. Three months of summer colour and nine months of nothingness seems to be missing opportunity after opportunity, so consider how you can use different types of plants to increase the usefulness of the window-boxes for a longer period.

**'Permanent' plantings** will last undisturbed for several years and should be attractive, if not particularly colourful, all the year round. You will need to depend largely on dwarf evergreen

Separate the plants if several have been grown together, and position the plants on top of the compost first to judge the spacing.

Plant carefully, making sure the hole is big enough, and firm the compost around the plants afterwards. Water thoroughly when planted.

shrubs and dwarf conifers, but that does not mean that the boxes have to be drab. There will be contrast of shape as well as colour in the form of grey-leaved plants, those with golden foliage, and of course many shades of green. Variegated small-leaved ivies will cascade down the front and with time will become a real feature.

Among the useful shrubs to try are *Aucuba japonica*, *Buxus sempervirens* 'Suffruticosa', *Euonymus fortunei*, small *Fatsia japonica*, *Hebe armstrongii*, *Hebe* × *franciscana* 'Variegata', and *Hebe pinguifolia* 'Pagei'. Even this short list can provide lots of useful combinations, but adding a few dwarf conifers will provide a welcome change of shape and form. A few useful for shape or colour are *Chamaecyparis lawsoniana* 'Ellwoodii', *C. pisifera* 'Boulevard', *Juniperus communis* 'Compressa', and *Thuja occidentalis* 'Rheingold'. You will find more suggestions in Chapter 8, but the plants mentioned so far, in combination with ivies to provide a trailing habit, will provide lots of interesting combinations for year-round interest.

Bear in mind, however, that all these plants will eventually outgrow a window-box, even though they may take many years to do so. They will in fact be dwarfed anyway by the restricted root-run (rather as a bonsai tree is dwarfed in a more extreme form). Feed only as often as it seems necessary to keep them looking healthy.

Window-boxes maintained by professionals sometimes include expendable shrubs such as Cape heaths *(Erica hiemalis)* and winter cherries *(Solanum capsicastrum* and its relatives), but these displays become very expensive. For the amateur these plants are best enjoyed indoors for their relatively brief display, and long-lasting shrubs used outdoors.

**Bulbs**  There are lots of early-flowering dwarf bulbs that you can use in a window-box. You will have a rather dull period while they are developing if you plant directly into the boxes, but you could grow the bulbs in pots and plunge these in the box as they come into flower; that way you could have a succession of bulbs by growing a range of different types and replacing them as the flowers die. Grow enough of each type to make a good display. Whether planting dwarf bulbs directly into the window-box or into pots, plant in generous groups close

Late winter, and the *Narcissus cyclamineus* hybrid 'Peeping Tom' is already in flower.

A window-box on a balcony, with trailing lobelia doing its usual good job of hiding the front. Petunias and nemesia are in the top – nemesia will soon run to seed and stop flowering if starved of food or water.

together, otherwise they will quite simply lack impact.

There is something to be said for planting directly into the boxes, especially with daffodils and tulips. You can pack more in by planting in two layers, one nestling above the other. This will give a bolder display, but for maximum effect it is best to keep to single subjects otherwise the flowers of one kind of bulb will be lost among the leaves of another at this close spacing.

There are dozens of *dwarf* bulbs that are suitable; really any that are dwarf and hardy, although it is best to avoid those that need time to become established (winter aconites, *Eranthis hyemalis*, for instance, are rather tricky to grow from dried corms in the first year and are likely to be disappointing until they become established).

Most trouble is likely to arise with daffodils, which seem a natural choice but can become a mess after the first strong wind. The wind has a buffeting effect against the wall, and tall daffodils will be forced forward and suffer the risk of broken stems even if staked (not easy in a window-box). Confine yourself to short varieties such as 'Jenny', 'Tête-a-Tête', or 'Peeping Tom', which are early and charming as well as compact.

Try planting a few spring-flowering bulbs in an evergreen window-box to add a little extra colour and interest. Window-boxes containing bulbs will usually be enhanced by a sprinkling of stone chippings over the surface, or in the case of plunged pots you can simply pack peat or pulverised bark between the pots and over the surface.

**Biennials** A neglected group, for the biennials (or plants treated as biennials) have a lot to offer in late winter and early spring. Wallflowers are a popular choice,

Mimulus are not traditional container plants, but the modern F1 hybrid varieties are suitable if you are prepared to dead-head them to keep the flowers coming. This variety is 'Malibu Orange'.

but not the best. Tall varieties really look rather ungainly, though of course you may be more interested in the fragrance. Compact varieties are much more suitable.

Winter-flowering pansies can make much prettier window-boxes and will flower earlier and for a longer period. Polyanthuses and primroses are also delightful container plants. Although these may be regarded as perennial plants, those for the window-box are best treated as a biennial crop; you can sow them yourself or buy young plants perhaps coming into flower. It is not a good idea to keep them in the window-box for another year, but you do not need to throw them away; just plant them in the garden.

The humble double daisy *(Bellis perennis)* in its many forms is worth planting either on its own or mixed with other plants, perhaps pansies.

**Bedding plants** This loose term covers a vast range of plants that flower in the summer (spring bedding plants have been discussed under biennials or bulbs). Most of them are seed-raised half-hardy annuals, although some tender perennials such as fuchsias and 'geraniums' (pelargoniums) are overwintered in a frost-free place. Seed-raised geraniums can be used, but generally those propagated vegetatively are still the most suitable for containers. Some of these are mentioned in the planting plans on pages 58–60, and many others will be found in Chapter 8.

Lobelia, fuchsias, petunias, geraniums and ivy in a plastic window-box.

## PLUNGE OR PLANT?

Many professional contractors that maintain window-boxes simply plunge the plants in peat rather than plant directly into compost. This is as much for convenience and the ability to modify the display easily as for the sake of the plants. Generally, for a long-term display it is best to plant into compost, the exception being very vigorous plants that may be better restrained in pots, even though the roots will eventually grow out into the compost through the drainage hole.

## PLANTING PLANS

These plans (pp. 58–60) are starting points, from which you can develop your own planting schemes. Even so you should use them with care; with shrubs and dwarf conifers especially you must be guided by the size of the plant when positioning them. The size of the box will also affect how many plants you can fit in, and their precise spacing, so always be prepared to modify your plan to take these points into account.

Note: these planting plans are not drawn to scale. Modify the spacing to suit the size of your box.

## SUMMER BOX

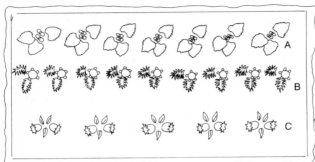

A    *Begonia semperflorens* or impatiens (compact variety)

B    Dwarf French marigolds (compact variety)

C    *Campanula isophylla* (blue form)

## YEAR-ROUND BOX

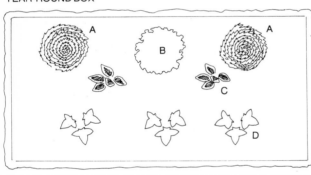

A    *Juniperus communis* 'Compressa'

B    *Thuja occidentalis* 'Rheingold'

C    *Euonymus fortunei* 'Emerald Gaiety'

D    Ivy

## YEAR-ROUND BOX

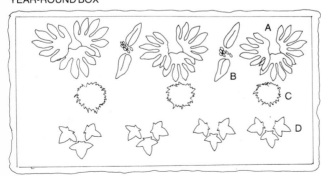

A    *Fatsia japonica*

B    *Aucuba japonica*

C    *Hebe × franciscana* 'Variegata'

D    Ivy

## YEAR-ROUND BOX

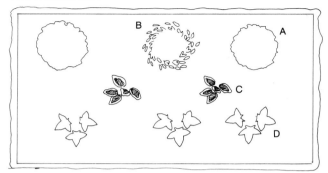

A *Chamaecyparis lawsoniana* 'Ellwoodii'

B *Santolina chamaecyparissus*

C *Euonymus fortunei* 'Emerald 'n' Gold'

D Ivy

## SPRING BOX

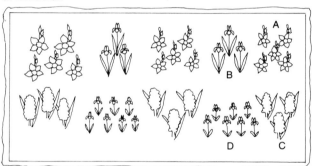

A *Narcissus* 'Tête-à-tête'

B *Iris reticulata*

C Hyacinths (blue)

D *Iris danfordiae*

## SPRING BOX

A Winter-flowering pansies

B Modern primoses

C Button-type *Bellis perennis*

## PERMANENT WITH SEASONAL VARIATION

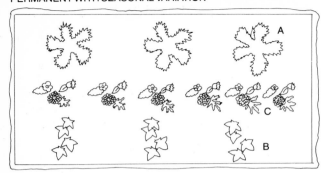

A   Hebe

B   Ivy

C   Change with season, such as polyanthus in spring, *Campanula carpatica* in summer, all-the-year-round chrysanthemums in autumn

## SUMMER BOX

A   Geraniums

B   Petunias

C   Lobelia (trailing)

## SUMMER BOX

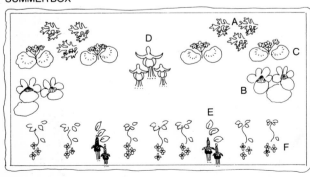

A   *Cineraria maritima*

B   Nasturtium (compact type)

C   Geranium

D   Fuchsia (upright)

E   Fuchsia (cascading)

F   Lobelia (trailing)

# 4·TUBS AND TROUGHS

Although this chapter bears the modest title tubs and troughs, it covers the rather grander vases, urns and jardinieres too. Whatever name the manufacturer gives to them, these containers should be looked upon in a far more creative way than window-boxes and hanging baskets. With baskets and window-boxes the emphasis has to be on getting the very best display of colour or foliage effect; the container itself is only a means of holding and displaying the plants.

Some of the containers in this chapter are decorative in their own right, and the way in which you arrange them in the garden, and with each other, can be almost as important as the plants. That is not to say that the plants do not need care, in selection and cultivation, but that sometimes they may need to take second place. This is not a garden design book, so the choice of urns and the like as mere ornaments is beyond the scope of this book. The containers discussed here are really intended to hold plants (or at least you can use them very effectively as plant containers), although their role in garden design has been mentioned in Chapter 1.

There are two prime considerations when choosing free-standing containers (for want of a better generic term) for the garden: how well they blend with your garden, and the type of plants that you intend to grow in them. You might add cost, but there is a way round this one; it is better to buy one good container that is really effective than three or four cheaper ones that do not really look right. If you merely want plant-holders, of course, and are not fussed about the aesthetics, then cost and suitability for the plants may be all you need to be concerned about.

Remember, however, that you need either spectacular plants or arresting containers. What you should endeavour to avoid is a mediocre or uninspiring container filled with far from inspiring plants. In other words, before you buy a container you need to have a good idea of how it is going to be *used*, and the pros and cons on the various materials and styles of container described in this chapter should always be considered in conjunction with particular needs and planting intentions.

## SHRUB TUBS

Shrub tubs should be considered as a need apart. They might well support the same shrub or small tree for five or ten years and even with careful choice of

61

A small selection of the many beautiful containers that are available in reconstituted stone or terracotta. There are plenty of elegant and interesting styles if you look for them.

plant (some suitable candidates are suggested below), it must have a long life and be suitable for the job.

Size and shape are as important as material. There are also design considerations that it is easy to overlook until you come across the problems. Adequate drainage is an obvious requirement (some plastic tubs do not have any), but the need for a rim to help when lifting may not be so obvious (remember that there

will be a considerable weight and it may not be easy to get a grip on a non-rimmed planted tub). You want good compost capacity, which can be deceptive with some shapes (check the actual capacity if possible – less than 20 litres/0.71 cu ft is not very generous). Some shapes (roughly barrel-shaped with a top that tapers inwards, for instance) may cause more than a degree of consternation if later you want to get the plant out to move it to a

Single-subject planting can often be more striking than a mixture, and using a single colour rather than a mixture can be particularly effective, as with these petunias.

larger container. By the time the roots have grown and filled the tub you may be left with something that will be much more difficult to get out than it was to put in.

## TROUGHS

With a window-box there are practical reasons why the dimensions and compost capacity may need to be small; space is usually restricted, and weight is likely to

A welcome at the door. If you have a light porch, make the most of it.

be a problem. With a trough that has firm ground for support, there is no excuse for inadequate capacity. Think carefully before you buy a trough less than about 23 cm (9 in) across and 20 cm (8 in) deep. Only if the container is particularly decorative in some way should you consider smaller dimensions, and then confine the planting to small annuals and dwarf bulbs, for instance. Bear in mind that most troughs sit on the ground, and you are generally looking down on them, so the plants may assume more importance than a particularly fine or delicate decoration. For that reason, a trough chosen for its fine figurines as decoration

may be best displayed nearer to eye level, perhaps on a low wall. You could, of course, raise a suitable trough on plinths, but for this to look right the materials must be compatible. A terracotta trough on reconstituted stone plinths is going to look rather hideous, whereas a reconstituted stone trough may look superb in the same situation.

## CONTAINERS FOR A SEASONAL DISPLAY

There are many small or shallow containers that would be unsuitable for shrubs, but are perfectly adequate for annuals and bulbs for instance. Dish-shaped containers can be shallow in the centre, and very shallow at the edges, but most seasonal bedding plants will cope with this quite happily provided you water them regularly. Urns and vases may have depth but a comparatively small surface area, and these may be best used as a general ornament just planted with seasonal plants to add interest (although they can be very effective planted with trailing plants such as ivies).

Hostas look good in containers, but they need lots of water to do well.

Pots will almost always be more effective grouped, unless the planting is very bold.

## STRAWBERRY POTS

This type of container is usually chosen because its shape appeals, and in the larger sizes they are obviously as much an ornament as a plant holder. Avoid the temptation to 'kill' the container by planting with gaudy or overpowering plants: let the planting be restrained. Strawberry pots can, however, be used merely as a plant-holder with the intention of completely covering the container with a mass of flowers. By planting a vigorous and bushy type of impatiens around the side as well as the top, you can create a mound of bloom that hides the pot (see page 110).

## MATERIALS

**Asbestos-cement** See window-boxes (page 39).

**Concrete** Many people shudder at the suggestion of concrete containers. Nevertheless, they are strong and many are well designed. Large concrete containers are also quite expensive. If the design really appeals but the container looks rather austere, you can use trailing plants round the edge to help soften the appearance. An old method of improving the appearance by speeding up nature's weathering is to paint the container with a mixture of cow dung and water. A solution of an

Fairly plain large terracotta pots are ideal for shrubs such as this variegated *Aucuba japonica*.

If you have a bold container it can make a bold focal point even without plants.

ordinary liquid fertiliser brushed on is perhaps a more acceptable suggestion. Concrete containers are useful for fairly substantial trees that offer a lot of wind resistance and need a firm, heavy base.

**Glass-reinforced cement** See window-boxes (page 41).

**Glass-reinforced plastic** See window-boxes (page 54).

**Lead** Lead containers have a really classic look, but they need an old-fashioned setting to look right (most are reproductions of antique containers). They are also heavy and expensive.

**Plastic** Some quite large shrub tubs are available in plastic (polypropylene or high-density polythene are the most common types). They are light, dry out less quickly than clay pots, and are not very expensive. Of course plastics can become brittle in sunlight after a couple of seasons, so check that it contains a UV (ultra-violet) inhibitor. Colour may also fade with time. Plastic containers are useful, but not a good investment if you want a container that will enhance your garden for a long time.

**Terracotta** Terracotta containers are not cheap and can be broken all too easily, so check what you are buying carefully to make sure that it is not cracked or damaged. Small cracks may let in moisture, which when frozen in winter may cause a fracture. You can try covering the pots with polythene in winter to keep them dry and so reduce the risk of frost damage, but the prospect of a garden full of polythene-wrapped pots is not an appealing one.

The plants do not have to be bold and brash to look good. Silver-leaved foliage plants can be particularly attractive in terracotta.

You need a large established fuchsia for this effect – you are unlikely to achieve this kind of result in one season from a young plant.

The problem in summer is that the pots dry out so rapidly, so it pays to concentrate on those plants that will not suffer unduly if the compost does become rather dry. You can reduce the speed with which the compost dries out by painting the inside of the container with a silicone-based water-repellent of the type used to deal with penetrating damp on brickwork.

**Timber** Large wooden containers look good with small trees, shrubs, and even suitable herbaceous plants. Some of them, such as half-barrels, provide a generous root-run. When buying a half-barrel, make sure that the metal hoops are tight (you can tighten the timber if it has shrunk by soaking it in water for about a week).

All wooden containers ought to be treated with a wood preservative of a kind not toxic to plants, such as one based on copper naphthanate. Sometimes, a white-painted wooden container can look particularly appealing, but of course you have to keep it looking clean and freshly painted if you embark on this course. The metal hoops on half-barrels will often benefit from rust-treatment and the use of an outdoor varnish. For wooden containers generally, oak, iroko, and teak are very durable woods. Avoid softwoods if possible.

## CHOOSING THE PLANTS

Summer bedding plants, from the ever-popular geraniums (good because they tolerate dry soil), to the much-loved petunias and other half-hardy annuals, need no special mention (you will find lots of them listed in Chapter 8), but you should be particularly careful not to mix too many plants or colours in the same container. Try to keep to one or two kinds of plants, in different colours if you like, or mix the plants but keep to a colour scheme (perhaps grey and pink, or green and gold). Avoid, if you can, too many different *kinds* of plants in different colours in the one container. Do not be afraid of single-subject planting either. Useful though seasonal bedding and bulbs can be, the majority of containers, especially tubs, should really have year-round interest from evergreens or other interesting shrubs.

**Evergreens for tubs** *Aucuba japonica* 'Crotonifolia' (spotted laurel), *Buxus sempervirens* (dwarf varieties of box), *Ilex* (holly), *Laurus nobilis* (sweet bay), *Lavandula* (lavender), *Rosmarinus* (rosemary).

**Conifers for tubs** *Chamaecyparis lawsoniana* 'Ellwoodii', *C. obtusa* 'Nana Gracilis', *Juniperus communis* 'Compressa', *J. horizontalis*, and *J. virginiana* 'Skyrocket'. A group of about three conifers of contrasting shape or colour can look good planted in the same container, but it needs to be large.

A simple contrast of white petunias and red geraniums, making a really eye-catching display.

A tiny front garden but a bright welcome at the door.

70

Daffodils in a cut-down barrel. Simple but a very welcome sight on a spring day.

A wooden container like this will support a good display because it holds a lot of compost.

An old lead container put to good use with a late spring display of pansies.

Pansies are particularly useful for enhancing an interesting container. This is an old stone trough.

Hostas in a decorated terracotta trough. These are very demanding plants to grow in a container of this kind because it is difficult to provide sufficient moisture.

Impatiens make superb container plants, and will do well in shade or full sun.

**Flowering shrubs** should not be overlooked, but pride of place must go to those that are also evergreen. Among those to consider are: camellias, *Choisya ternata,* and rhododendrons (the *R. yakushimanum* hybrids are particularly good).

**Tender shrubs** are a possibility for your patio, especially as you can take them in for the winter (into a greenhouse if available, into the home if not). Of course you have to be prepared to move the possibly

Dwarf conifers can make pleasant container plants, but you need to use interesting containers.

If you are fortunate enough to have an interesting old container, try to make a real focal point of it.

very heavy containers around. For fun you could try citrus fruits such as grapefruit, lemons and oranges; or choose something with a fairly exotic reputation such as oleander *(Nerium oleander)*.

## SHRUBS WITH FORM

Especially valuable in the right sort of container to set them off well are the 'architectural' plants that have a shape or habit that makes them particularly useful as focal points or to give shape and form to an otherwise uninteresting corner. A large agave can look very striking (and can be left out in winter in favourable areas); some palms are tough; and yuccas look tender but will do well in all but the very unfavourable areas. The fan palm *Trachycarpus fortunei* and *Cordyline australis* are reasonably hardy and may be worth a try, even if you need to give them some winter protection in cold districts. Hardier, and very popular, is *Fatsia japonica* (the false castor oil plant), which is worth a place in any garden.

## REMEMBER THE BULBS

If you decide to plant deciduous trees in tubs, plant early-flowering spring bulbs around the edge of the container. They will provide a welcome break during the dormant season.

A useful device for bringing interest to the base of a container. The plants round the base are grape hyacinths *(Muscari armeniacum)*.

A reconstituted stone ornament. You need the right setting for a container of this scale.

# 5·OTHER CONTAINERS

An enthusiastic 'container gardener' is not likely to be restricted by what the manufacturers care to produce; all kinds of potential containers can be pressed into use, from long-discarded lavatories to the pensioned-off wheelbarrow. Where ordinary garden space is at a premium you may want to grow as many plants as possible in a limited and unpromising space, and the actual container is less important than the mere provision of a growing medium. For the latter, growing bags may be ideal, unattractive though they sound for decorative effect. Some of the suggestions in this chapter will either appal or appeal; it is all a matter of your idea of what gardening is about.

## GROWING BAGS

Growing bags are purely functional; a few may have coloured flowers and vegetables printed on the sides but this simply makes them look more appealing in the shop and does little to enhance the garden. To dismiss growing bags purely in terms of appearance is, however, to miss out on a most useful type of container gardening.

If you want to grow vegetables in containers, growing bags are ideal for a wide range of plants from lettuces and radishes to tomatoes, and can give surprising results with vegetables as unlikely as carrots and potatoes. The vegetable-growing possibilities are discussed in more detail on pages 124–126.

Growing bags make a good home for bedding plants on a balcony, especially where they can be viewed from below so that the flowers are seen but not the bags. Once the flowers are in full bloom, you should not in fact see much of the bags anyway. A bag full of petunias, or perhaps impatiens, will look spectacular.

Growing bags can also be used for a wide range of flowers and in many situations if you are prepared to regard them as gap-fillers. You could, for instance plant your previous year's (new) growing bags with compact-growing bulbs for a spring display. As you will only want to move the bag into position to brighten up a dull spot as the bulbs come into bloom, it is best to place the bag on a board so that it can be moved more easily when the time comes.

For 'greedy' crops such as tomatoes, it is best to buy new bags each year, but you can then relegate them to providing a

Planting fibrous-rooted begonias in a growing bag.

Growing bags are useful for flowers as well as vegetables. This one uses compressed peat that has to be expanded before you plant.

Water poured on to the bag expands the compost. Even ordinary growing bags should have the compost moistened before you plant.

An old wooden wheelbarrow put to good use. It is surprising what a coat of paint can do to improve the appearance of an old barrow.

An inverted chimney-pot planted with geraniums.

home for things like lettuces, radishes, or bulbs, and bedding annuals for another season. After that it is best to use the peat to improve the soil elsewhere in the garden.

## 'STONE' SINKS

Most of the genuine old stone sinks have long since been broken up or sold off at highly inflated prices. Glazed sinks can be pressed into use by giving them a coating of 'hypertufa' (see below), but the greater depth of these sinks seldom makes them such an attractive proposition.

You can make a 'hypertufa' coating by mixing 1 part coarse sand or fine grit, 1 part cement, and 2 parts damp, sieved peat, mixed dry first then with water into a doughy consistency.

To coat a glazed sink, first clean it thoroughly, making sure it is free of grease and dirt, then try to score the glaze outside and down into the top few inches inside as best you can with a coarse file (a job that is not as easy as some would have you believe).

Then paint the same area with a PVA adhesive and allow it to become tacky (it should take about 10 minutes). *Using waterproof gloves,* slap on a layer of the hypertufa mix, pressing it firmly against the sink. This is a messy job but somehow quite satisfying.

This was an old metal table before it was converted into a useful plant holder (right).

Old tyres put to good use. White emulsion paint will do much to transform their appearance. Insert a bucket in the top if you want to reduce the amount of compost needed to fill the cavity.

Take the hypertufa over the rim and down into the inside far enough to take the coating beyond compost level. A thickness of 12 mm (½ in) should be adequate. Make sure the sink is kept frost-free until the mixture has set hard. Once the mixture has dried out, you can accelerate the weathering by brushing on a solution of an ordinary liquid fertiliser.

*A word of warning* before you embark on this job: do it as near as possible to the place that you will use the sink. An *empty* glazed sink can be very heavy, and by the time you add a layer of concrete it will need a couple of people to move it safely. If possible, it is worth trying to do the job *in situ.* If you do, raise the sink on a couple of bricks first, so that there will be free drainage beneath once the sink has been planted.

## MAKING YOUR OWN CONCRETE SINK

There is an alternative to trying to improve the appearance of an old glazed

An old stone sink planted with alpines. At ground level much of its impact might be lost; using plinths makes much more of a feature of it.

This was an old wire mesh litter bin, now it makes an ideal home for a mass display of fibrous-rooted begonias.

sink: make a concrete trough from scratch. This actually has a lot to commend it, because you can make it to more acceptable proportions. Just follow the step-by-step instructions below.

1) Make a 2.5 cm (1 in) bed of moist sand, larger than the finished trough, with a firm and flat surface. On this you can lay a number of bricks on edge, eight bricks giving you a trough with an inside area of about 45 × 30 cm (18 × 12 in), and cover them with a sheet of polythene, tucking it in neatly under the edges.

2) Then mould the damp sand to form a smooth, curved channel around the bricks (this will form the rim of the trough, so bear that in mind when deciding on the width of the channel).

3) Using a concrete mix of 3 parts sand to 1 part cement (you can use a cement dye to give it a sandstone colour if you wish), trowel the concrete around the bricks, firming it up the sides. If the mixture is too wet it will not cling to the polythene on the sides.

4) Make sure the top of the bricks are covered with 12 mm (½ in) of concrete too, and use a float trowel to smooth the concrete.

5) For strength you will have to reinforce the concrete with wire-netting cut to a rectangle that covers the base and overlaps the sides by about 7.5 cm (3 in). You will need to fold this round the shape carefully, being particularly careful to get neat corners. It should lie flat against the

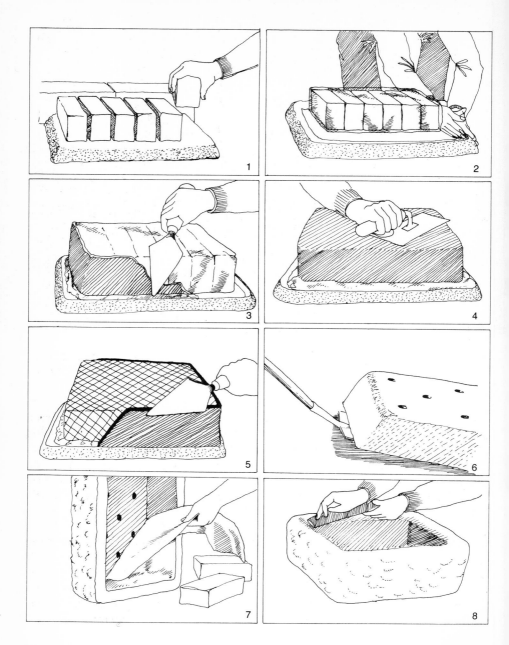

1

2

3

4

5

6

7

8

82

An old manger in a new role. It has been lined with wire-netting to hold in the moss and compost.

concrete, then you can cover it with another layer of concrete to give a final thickness of about 4 cm (1½ in), which should again be smoothed.

6) Drainage is essential, so bore at least five 2.5 cm (1 in) holes through the base before the concrete sets. You will also need to scrub the surface with a stiff brush after about 24 hours, when the concrete has partially set, to produce a matt, more stone-like finish.

7) It will take about four days for the concrete to set hard enough to risk lifting the trough by sliding a spade under the edge and lifting. It should lift clear of the bricks and then the polythene can be pulled off.

8) For the finishing touches, make sure the drainage holes are clear, and round off the edges with a coarse file or shaping tool (do this before the concrete becomes too hard). Finally, hose it down, scrubbing it with a stiff brush. If necessary, you can accelerate weathering by brushing on a diluted liquid fertiliser.

## A LIGHTER OPTION

Making a concrete trough is heavy work. For say a balcony or roof garden you may not want such weight anyway. There is a lightweight alternative that you can make from a block of expanded polystyrene (which you should be able to buy from a good builder's merchant).

1) Saw the block to the approximate finished size first, then using a combination of saws and knives hack out the centre of the block, being careful not to go too deep and jeopardise the strength of the trough.

2) You will need the walls to be as thick as possible for strength, but thin for the sake of appearance, so it is worth tapering them so that they are thinner at the top and thicker towards the base. If you want to round the edges this is easy to do with a shaping tool, but be careful not to

An old tyre has been used to provide a small raised bed around a young tree. This can be planted with spring bulbs followed by summer bedding, or you could plant with more permanent carpeting shrubs.

overdo it. Remember to make adequate drainage holes – you can drill them out or cut them out with a knife.

3) Use a PVA adhesive to coat the outside and part way down the inside.

4) When tacky, press on a coating of coarse grit. If it is not too coarse you should be able to coat it thickly enough to hide the polystyrene.

*Be warned:* sawing and shaping expanded polystyrene is a messy job (the bits fly everywhere), so the garden is a better place than indoors for this job. To avoid putting strain on the finished container, do not fill it with compost until it is in position.

## PLANTING A TROUGH OR SINK

Although sink gardens can be used for other dwarf plants (pansies can look good, for instance), they look their best with alpines, perhaps decorated with a few pieces of rock too.

If you are an alpine enthusiast you will know of hundreds of good alpines that will be suitable, but for a non-specialist a short, uncomplicated list of plants is often more useful as a starting point. The following plants, described in more detail in Chapter 8, are good candidates: *Achillea* 'King Edward', *Aethionema* 'Warley Rose', *Androsace chumbyi*, *Arabis ferdinandi-coburgi* 'Variegata', *Campanula carpatica*, *Cyclamen hederifolium* (*C. neapolitanum*), *Gentiana acaulis*, *Geranium cinereum subcaulescens*, *Hepatica nobilis (H. triloba)*, *Hypericum olypicum*, *Lewisia* 'Rose Splendour', *Leontopodium alpinum*, *Phlox douglasii*, *Rhodohypoxis baurii*, *Raoulia australis*, *Saxifraga paniculata (S. aizoon)* 'Rosea' (and many other saxifragas), *Sedum lydium*, *Sedum spathulifolium* 'Purpureum', *Sempervivum tectorum* (and many other sempervivums).

## SOME LESS USUAL CONTAINERS

The possibility of suitable containers is limited only by the imagination. For those who like to put old household fittings to good use, old coal scuttles, lavatories, and even the old bath, may be pressed into use, though you have to be

Plants in ordinary pots usually lack appeal, but on this display stand the result is very pleasing.

Gazanias in a terracotta container. These plants need a very sunny position.

careful about the image these things bring to your garden. For a bit of humour they are fine. But for a keen gardener concerned about their place within the garden setting, they would probably be a distracting gimmick.

Gardeners often find old garden utensils more appealing. Old watering-cans, and of course the ever-popular wheelbarrow, somehow have a more acceptable image even in a 'gardener's garden'.

The choice of unusual containers can also reflect an area or type of community. At a fishing port you may find lifeboat covers (bath-like objects for the non-nautical among us), and even old fishermen's boots can be pressed into use (see illustration on page 10).

Old-fashioned chimney-pots also have their supporters. These are occasionally offered for sale in garden centres, but if you happen to have a demolition site close to hand you should be able to obtain them very much cheaper.

There are hundreds of other objects that could be used, including cut-down plastic bottles and containers, but temper the urge to try the novel or unusual with an awareness of the effect on the tone of your garden!

## PLANTING A TUB OR TROUGH

All containers need good drainage, and an inch of material that will encourage water to drain away freely is a good starting point. You will of course have to cover large drainage holes with pieces of broken clay pots or slate, or even broken polystyrene tiles, but the days when gardeners had enough broken crocks around the garden to provide a whole drainage layer have gone. Just as good, once the actual holes have been protected, is gravel or even coarse grit.

Suitable composts are suggested in Chapter 6, but avoid the temptation to use ordinary garden soil. It is not worth the disappointment, having spent money on buying the containers and the plants, that almost inevitably results from using ordinary garden soil.

If you are planting bedding plants or alpines, or anything with a small root-ball, it is sufficient to fill the container loosely with compost to within about 2.5 cm (1 in) of the rim, then make planting holes with a trowel. When planting, make sure the root-ball is well firmed into the compost, which should just cover the root-ball so that it does not remain exposed to dry out.

Trees and shrubs need more careful planting. Add enough compost to bring the top of the root-ball about 2.5 cm (1 in) below the rim of the container, then tease out some roots from the base of the root-ball (it is always best to buy container-grown plants for this job), and spread them out before gradually packing more compost around the plants. If the roots are tightly matted around the sides of the root-ball too, it may be worth teasing a few of these out too.

# 6·WATERING AND FEEDING

Although this chapter is headed Watering and Feeding, the first thing to consider is compost. Subsequent feeding, and to a lesser extent watering advice, is influenced by the compost that you use. Plants growing in containers are at a tremendous disadvantage over plants growing in open ground. Their root-run is confined, so the plants cannot send roots down or out further in search of nutrients or moisture, and in a container that is heavily planted there will be much competition between plants for what is there. To give the plants a chance to do well, you really do have to take seriously both the compost and the routines of feeding and watering. Neglect any one of these points and you are unlikely to grow good container plants.

## THE COMPOST

Nowadays loamless composts predominate. They are light, 'clean', and easy to use, and generally more agreeable for us to handle. Sadly they are not the complete answer, especially for containers. They can be difficult to rewet properly if they dry out too much (which they can easily do if you are not careful), may quickly run out of food for an intensively-planted container, and lack the weight and stability necessary for some of the larger plants in say tubs. John Innes and other loam-based composts are unfortunately heavy, which can be a very considerable problem for hanging baskets, and may also be undesirable for window-boxes.

By mixing equal parts of a loam-based compost such as John Innes potting compost No. 3 and a peat-based potting or all-purpose compost, you should have the best of both worlds: a compost that has a better natural reservoir of nutrients, and that is less disastrous if the container does become dry, with less weight than a loam-based compost alone, and with peat to absorb and retain moisture that is there.

This is a good compost mixture to use for hanging baskets and window-boxes. You can also use it to advantage in other containers of course, but for many troughs and tubs either a good loam-based compost *or* a peat-based one should be perfectly acceptable. For shrubs and small trees in tubs, however, it is probably best to use a loam-based compost as this will support a long-term plant better than a peat compost, and the extra weight will be a necessary anchor during strong winds. At the time of writing, a 'hanging basket' compost has been announced by a compost manufacturer that incorporates the basic principles of the loam-peat mixture described. If you can find this sort of compost it will save you the job of mixing your own.

There are compost additives that you could consider. Products such as vermiculite and perlite are well known, might help, and certainly will not do any harm. They will not make routine care such as regular watering and feeding any less necessary.

Among other products that you could try adding if you want to experiment are pulverised bark and polystyrene beads (though you may have difficulty in obtaining the latter).

Perhaps far more interesting are the 'superabsorbent polymer' additives. These are water-retaining gels that enable the compost to retain moisture without waterlogging. At the time of writing these are only just becoming available to amateurs so it is early to be sure how beneficial these will be. Some scientific trials have suggested that they are by no means an answer to all your watering problems, but they are probably going to be useful for plants normally under water stress in good light conditions − hanging baskets for instance.

The exact method of use depends on the product, but typically a sachet of the crystals is poured into a bucket containing 2.25 litres (4 pints) of water, left for a couple of hours, then mixed with ten times the volume of potting compost. Do not expect miracles, but it is probably worth a try for all containers, in particular hanging baskets.

Compost additives that might help to ease the problem of water-retention. From left to right: vermiculite, perlite, and two brands of superabsorbent polymers. It is worth trying any of these as an additive, but if possible grow a similar container without the additive alongside, so that you can judge any benefits for yourself.

## FEEDING

If you use peat-based compost alone, it is best to start feeding after about three weeks. Although the nutrient levels will depend on the brand of compost it is well worth feeding after three weeks to be on the safe side, that is assuming that you have not added a slow-release fertiliser to the compost. Some experts do not think that slow-release fertilisers are a good thing for containers such as hanging baskets, as in theory there can be a build-up of salts. In practice there is a lot of evidence that they do very well for hanging baskets and other containers too; they are widely used by professionals.

Brands may come and go, but you should ask at your garden centre for a slow-release fertiliser. There are several types; some come as pellets or sticks that you push into the compost, others as granules that you can mix with the compost. The granules are probably the first choice, but failing that you could use the other types. Some might be sold as slow-release houseplant fertilisers, but they are equally suitable for your hanging basket or greenhouse pot plants.

It is important to appreciate that slow-release fertilisers are specially formulated to release nutrients over a period of many months (at least three). Those affected by temperature will only release the plant foods when the weather is warm enough for plant growth.

Various trials have suggested better results with these than using liquid feeds.

There is an even more compelling reason for amateurs to consider them: once a slow-release is used the plants are sure to be fed; with a liquid feed it depends on how conscientiously it is applied. Liquid feeding will still remain popular of course, and it can be successful if done consistently and methodically. That is far more important than using a particular brand. It makes sense to feed on a particular day, maybe every Saturday or Sunday, so that you remember more easily.

Never under-rate the importance of feeding plants in containers, but avoid falling into the trap of assuming that giving more than the recommended dose will make them even better. It can have the opposite effect because excess salts can build up in the compost and actually inhibit growth.

## WATERING

Watering is the biggest drawback to container gardening. It is quite simply a chore. It is time-consuming (even with a hose-pipe) and extremely laborious if you have to use a watering-can. The problem is compounded when it comes to the inaccessibility of hanging baskets. In the height of summer it is a problem that you have to turn your attention to *daily*, even

A self-watering window-box or trough. Although intended primarily for indoor use, this type can also be used equally well outdoors. They are, however, relatively expensive.

though you would probably rather go down to the beach instead. During your summer holidays you will need to make arrangements for someone to do the watering. Watering is not only the biggest drawback to container gardening, it is also the problem least easy to solve.

There are drip-feed automatic watering systems for greenhouses, which could be adapted for outdoors, and there are irrigation systems intended specifically for outdoor use, where the water seeps out of special hoses. However, none of these are really a solution to lots of containers dotted around different parts of the garden. Nor would you particularly want a network of hoses and tubing cascading around your plants. So it comes back primarily to the watering-can or hose-pipe.

For one or two containers a watering-can may be perfectly satisfactory, but the more containers that you have the more a hose-pipe is justified. The problem with a hose-pipe is the chore of getting it out, fixing it on the tap, perhaps dealing with drips and leaks, and putting it away afterwards. Invest in an outside tap, with a screw fitting (which is less likely to drip than many other fittings), and have a hose-reel on the wall close by. If you can afford a through-feed hose-reel, so that you just pull off as much hose as you need to, and turn on the tap, this will be a good investment.

Fold-flat hoses that you can reel up into a small holder sound good, but they are not without problems. Some have a nasty habit of kinking when you go round a corner or move the hose at an awkward angle, and reeling them in again is not always the easy and trouble-free task that it is made out to be.

Hanging baskets are undoubtedly the most awkward to water, and because they are so exposed are likely to need watering the most frequently. Anyone who has tried watering a hanging basket with a watering-can knows the problems; sleeves get wet even if you use a long spout. For one or two baskets a milk-bottle may be one solution, but for several a hose-pipe still makes life easier.

There are in fact basket lances that you can fit to a hose-pipe, and several that can be fitted to a compression sprayer. These are actually quite good: you pump up the pressure and a stream of water is delivered to the basket through the angled lance when you press the trigger. This is an effort perhaps worthwhile for one or two baskets, but still a bind if you have a lot. If you have a compression sprayer it is worth buying one of these to see whether you find it useful.

Some people solve the problem by popping a few ice-cubes into the basket each day. They dissolve slowly to release the water and there are of course few drips from the basket. If this sounds easier than taking out a milk-bottle of water, it is worth a try.

## Self-watering containers and tanks

To anyone with lots of containers the word 'self-watering' sounds like a dream. It is one that is easily shattered. The number of truly self-watering containers

is strictly limited. Most are intended for indoor use, and although there is a practical self-watering trough designed primarily for indoor use that can also be used outside it is not much help unless you want a plastic window-box of those dimensions. These are quite expensive, but if they suit your particular need, and you are prepared to pay the price, they should work well.

Self-watering hanging baskets should be treated with some scepticism. Of those available to amateurs at the time of writing most have little more than a means of catching some excess water that can be drawn back into the compost later. It takes courage to depend on this, so you may end up watering regularly anyway.

There are various forms of lance for watering hanging baskets. Some fit a normal hose-pipe, others fit widely-available compression sprayers. A watering lance is well worth considering if you have several baskets to water, otherwise the effort of getting out special equipment may not be worthwhile. A through-feed hose reel and an outside tap can be invaluable if you have a lot of containers of any kind.

Self-watering tanks appear to have much more potential. There are small ones holding 1 litre (1¾ pints) for a hanging basket and larger ones for boxes and troughs. The principle is sound: you insert them into the container before filling with compost, leaving the filling spout just above the surface. Capillary action draws water from the reservoir.

The drawback is that they take up

A self-watering tank suitable for a window-box or trough. Bear in mind that although there will be a reservoir of water you lose valuable compost space.

valuable space. In a very large container they may be worth considering, but in a small trough the tank could take up a good proportion of the space that would otherwise be used for compost, and this could cause problems. They are least use in hanging baskets, where the tank will take up so much room that there is hardly any space left for compost once you allow for the root-balls. You may also find it impossible to fit a large plant into the

centre of the basket. Add to that the problem of knowing whether the tank needs topping up and the difficulty of adding the water through a small spout without lifting the basket down each time, and the hose-pipe will probably seem preferable.

Mulching containers is not as silly as it sounds, and it may help to reduce water loss. Window-boxes and tubs are the obvious candidates. Moist peat is a popular choice, but pulverised bark can look more attractive and even gravel can be used as a decorative mulch. Although mulching will not remove the problem of watering, it may reduce the risk of the compost drying out too quickly.

# 7·OTHER MAINTENANCE

Regular watering and feeding are the main essentials for successful container displays, but there are 'finishing touches' that will ensure your containers look smart and the plants remain looking good too. It is only common sense to deal with pests and diseases as soon as they are noticed, but to get the best from your plants many of them will also need 'grooming': dead-heading, shaping, and perhaps training. If you have good-looking plants it makes sense to keep the containers in good condition too.

## GROOMING

**Dead-heading** often helps to prolong the flowering period, though it is not a practical proposition with many plants. You could hardly dead-head lobelia or busy Lizzies (impatiens) for example, but where the seed heads are large, and not too numerous, it is usually worth going over the plants at least once a week to pinch off faded flowers and developing seed heads. Pansies and mimulus are typical of the plants that will benefit from this treatment. It not only helps to prevent the plants putting their energies into producing seed rather than more flowers but it also tidies up the plant.

With some plants the seed heads and dying flowers look very unattractive. The large heads of double begonias and African marigolds turn brown and will often start to rot; if not removed they spoil the effect of the flowers still

Late spring frosts and biting winds can damage the young emerging leaves of vulnerable plants such as Japanese maples.

Permanently-planted containers are best top-dressed each spring. Remove the top inch or so of compost from around the plants, and replenish with fresh compost.

Regular dead-heading will do much to improve the quality and length of display.

opening. It is worth spending time tidying up these plants. Plants like this are well worth dead-heading promptly.

Healthy plants should not have too many dead or yellowing leaves unless it is the end of the season. Any that appear are best removed to improve appearances and reduce the risk of disease.

**Pruning and shaping** can be as necessary for annuals as it is for shrubs. Shrubs in containers should be pruned in the same way as shrubs in other parts of

the garden; the exact technique depends on the plant, when it flowers, and whether it blooms on new wood or old. In addition to normal pruning, shrubs in tubs may also need shaping to make them neater and to keep them within bounds. Cutting back sprawling old wood may give a container shrub a new lease of life and delay the time when it has to be relegated to the garden and replaced with a fresh plant.

Do not be afraid to use the secateurs on shrubs such as box and bay if you want to shape them into globes, pyramids or whatever. This kind of shaping is best done by clipping little and often until you produce the right shape. Once shaped, routine clipping, perhaps with shears, will be adequate (secateurs are best used for large-leaved plants, otherwise half-cut leaves will turn brown and spoil the effect).

Bedding plants may need shaping too, but of course nothing more than a finger and thumb are needed. Pinching out the growing tip while the plant is still small is often all that is needed to encourage bushiness. Not all plants need it of course.

Climbers and trailers are a particular problem, and can easily look untidy rather than attractive. Climbers are generally better planted in the ground. Climber/trailers like black-eyed Susan (*Thunbergia alata*) will inevitably want to go up as well as down. With a plant like this it is best to disentangle stems that are scrambling upwards through the other plants and carefully drape them over the edge of the container − hanging baskets are an exception: here they will look very attractive scrambling up the chains or wires, and can make an attractive basket plant on their own. In a window-box, if you must have them scrambling upwards, try using the miniature trellises that you can buy for climbing pot-plants, keeping these to the back of the box.

Some climber/trailers are so vigorous that you simply have to make sure they cascade, otherwise they will take over the window-box. Climbing nasturtiums are an example, and you will have to pinch out any stems that threaten to engulf any other plants in a basket, for instance. Really, these long trailing varieties are best avoided; there are compact varieties that are much better suited to container growing.

---

## PESTS AND OTHER PROBLEMS

Most gardening books have a fairly extensive section on pests and diseases. Plants are vulnerable to the same pests and diseases in containers as they are in the ground, so this book will not attempt to describe what greenflies, grey mould, or slugs and snails look like; the chances are you already know. You are no more likely to encounter an uncommon pest or disease on a plant in your window-box or hanging basket than you are in the garden in general. What is important is how you control them.

Aphids of various kinds (greenfly, blackfly, and so on) are the most likely problem, and unfortunately the population can build up very rapidly in the summer, when a lot of damage can be done if you do not act promptly. On non-edible crops systemic insecticides are particularly useful because they offer more lasting protection, and insects that may be missed with a contact insecticide because of the dense growth will still be caught when they suck the sap. One or other of the systemic insecticides should control almost all of the sap-sucking or leaf-eating insects, though some kill different pests better than others.

New products will undoubtedly appear

Frost damage to a choisya.

during the life of this book, so specific chemicals are not suggested. Your garden shop should be able to tell you which are systemic (the label will almost certainly indicate this too). Most are liquids that

you spray on, but you can also buy sticks that you push into the compost which gradually release a chemical that is absorbed by the roots and in due course kills the insects. Although intended primarily for houseplants, these are a convenient way of dealing with pests in just a couple of containers if you do not want to mix a spray specially.

Aerosol insecticides are ideal for the home and have a use in the greenhouse, but outdoors you may not get such good cover because the fine droplets are so easily blown by the wind. They are also much more expensive than using sprays.

Sometimes you will encounter pests that are not so easily controlled by the normal systemic insecticides, and you may have to use other dusts or sprays; but always check the small print on the label. Some popular container plants may be damaged by certain insecticides. Dimethoate (one of the systemics) should not be used on begonias, fuchsias or salvias among other plants; malathion is not suitable for antirrhinums or petunias, for example. The assortment of plants that you have in say a window-box or hanging basket may dictate which insecticide is the most suitable.

Diseases should be less troublesome. The most likely problems are mildew and botrytis (grey mould) where plants are packed closely together with little air circulation. Good routine hygiene (picking off affected leaves or flowers as soon as they are noticed) will do a lot to control the problem, otherwise one of the modern fungicides in conjunction with hand-picking should bring the problem under control.

Slugs and snails can have a devastating effect, even overnight in a newly-planted container. It is no use hoping that they will not make it to a window-box, or be able to gain access to a hanging basket.

Nasturtiums are well known for attracting blackfly.

Somehow they seem to get anywhere, probably carried on the plants. Fortunately they are very easily controlled in containers with slug pellets.

Woodlice, sometimes called pillbugs, are almost certain to be encountered; they love to lurk in the dark, damp conditions that prevail beneath most containers. They will not usually do established plants much harm, but you will probably want to keep them under control. There are many dusts that you can buy, such as those based on gamma-HCH, that you can puff beneath the containers.

Plants may also look sickly or unhealthy for reasons other than pests or diseases. Pale, sickly-looking, yellowing leaves may simply mean that the plant needs feeding. Wind can also be devastating for some tender plants, especially in hanging baskets that are perhaps hung near a draughty corner (sometimes the leaves may shrivel or even become torn and tattered).

Bear in mind that lime-hating plants such as camellias, many heathers, and rhododendrons may have yellowing leaves and be growing poorly because there is too much lime in the compost (you should buy a special 'ericaceous' compost for these). You can try treating them with a chelated iron (sequestrene), but a better long-term solution is to repot them. One tremendous advantage of growing these shrubs in containers is that you can give them the right conditions even if your garden soil is unsuitable.

## PREPARING FOR WINTER

If you have a valuable terracotta pot it may be worth moving it into the greenhouse if possible, or if only used for summer bedding into the garden shed. They should stand heavy frosts, but accidents do sometimes happen if moisture has managed to seep into fine cracks. Sometimes the less robust overwintering trees and shrubs can be damaged if the compost becomes saturated and then frozen. You could try tying a sheet of polythene over the top of the container to prevent the compost becoming too wet, but you will need to check periodically to make sure the compost is not too dry.

## TOPDRESSING

Trees and shrubs have to grow in the same compost for many years. It is worth removing the top couple of inches of compost each spring and replacing it with fresh compost. Give this a miss if the container is also planted with perennials around the base.

# 8·THE PLANTS

Mention window-boxes or hanging baskets to most people and the plants they will probably suggest first will include 'geraniums' and fuchsias. That is not only because they are widely planted but because they are also very good container plants; quite simply they 'do well'. Of course there are hundreds of other possibilities, many of which will be just as successful though they are less commonly used. There is an even bigger group of plants that make good container plants if they have the right care and conditions.

The plants suggested on the following pages range from the fairly foolproof to the more challenging but worthwhile outdoor container plants. It is intended to provide the complete beginner with plenty of easy and reliable plants, while at the same time including some more exciting possibilities and challenges for the more experienced.

This chapter is not intended to be read through from beginning to end, but to be scanned to find suitable plants to consider. For that reason after the name for each entry you will find a list of uses and merits that should help you to narrow down the choice. The stars after each plant name indicate its worth, as follows:

\*\*\* tough and dependable;
 \*\* easy but needs care;
  \* can be tricky, but results make the challenge worthwhile. It is best if you have some experience of growing plants in containers.

Often it makes little difference which variety you choose, but sometimes variety can be important where it has qualities that make it particularly suitable for growing in containers. This has been indicated where it applies, and a suitable variety suggested (but bear in mind that new or existing equally suitable varieties may also be available).

## BULBS

Bulbs are at their most successful in troughs and window-boxes, but do not overlook the possibility of planting early-flowering bulbs in tubs containing shrubs or deciduous trees. They are not a sensible proposition for a hanging basket; good spring-flowering bulb baskets have been made, but it is very difficult to get the various bulbs in flower together. It is best to be content with planting a few bulbs, such as hyacinths or crocuses, in a mixed winter basket containing ivies and perhaps a few primroses.

*Anemone blanda* − sometimes disappointing for the first year, but easy and successful if left to become established.

### Anemone blanda* *Uses* Tub; trough.

This carpeting anemone with its usually blue daisy-like flowers is not difficult to grow once it has become established, but results are often disappointing from dry corms. Well worth planting in a permanent tub, where they can be left undisturbed, perhaps around a small tree, but for first-season display they can be very disappointing and it is best to grow the corms in pots (plant close together) and move them into the box or trough once they have grown and flowers are forming.

### Crocus, large-flowered*** *Uses* Trough; window-box.

Although there are very early species, such as *C. chrysanthus*, the flowers are really too small and delicate for a bold or eye-catching display. The large-flowered Dutch-type are best for containers.

### Eranthis hyemalis (winter aconite)* *Uses* Tub.

The bright and cheerful flowers in late winter are among the first flowers of the year, so are worth some effort just for that. They do not grow well from dry tubers, and need to be left undisturbed to form large clumps. Worth trying round the base of a tree or shrub in a tub, but mulch well each year.

*Hyacinth* 'Jan Bos' – all hyacinths make superb container plants, indoors or out.

### Hyacinths*** *Uses* Tub; trough; window-box.

Superb container plants, they can however easily be spoilt by planting in a single regimented row. They are most effective in bold clumps. It is best not to mix varieties within the same container as flowering times might not coincide.

### Iris danfordiae*** *Uses* Trough; window-box.

This is a plant that flowers in late winter, is fragrant (albeit not strongly so), cheerful yellow, is easy to grow, and must be on a shortlist of the most useful bulbs. Plant them close together for good impact. They are good in a window-box because you can appreciate the flowers and fragrance more easily.

### Iris reticulata*** *Uses* Trough; window-box.

A good investment, this iris is almost sure to give a good display the first year, and will go on multiplying in the garden for years to come. There are several varieties, in various shades of blue and even purple. *I. histrioides* is very similar.

### Muscari armeniacum (grape hyacinth)*** *Uses* Tub; trough; window-box.

These plants are very easy to grow, and

if you can leave them undisturbed will make increasingly large clumps. The leaves appear long before autumn sets in if left in the ground. They are useful in any container, but best planted around shrubs in tubs where they can be left. They can be effective interplanted with daffodils.

### Narcissus cyclamineus*** *Uses*
Trough; window-box.

The varieties that are most suitable are in fact the *N. cyclamineus* hybrids such as 'February Gold', and 'Peeping Tom'. Most of these hybrids grow to about

Giving a trough a white finish will often make more of a feature of it.

23–30 cm (9–12 in) and flower in late winter or early spring. Their shorter stems coupled with early flowering make them a much better proposition than the more traditional daffodils for most containers. The species itself is more suitable for a sink garden.

### Narcissus, large-flowered*** *Uses*
Tub.

The large-flowered narcissi (including the trumpet daffodils) are best confined to tubs. They can look particularly good in a half-barrel. For impact plant only one variety in each container, and plant them closely so that they provide a good display and help to support each other.

### Nerine bowdenii* *Uses* Trough.

This is one of the few good autumn-flowering bulbs for containers. Other autumn-flowering bulbs, such as colchicums and *Crocus speciosus* have to be massed very close together to make a decent first-year display, and even then it is fleeting. The nerines make such a superb and long-lasting display that it is worth persevering. They need a deep trough, and if you live in a cold area it may need moving to a cold greenhouse or given other form of protection, but after a season or two they should settle down and flower well.

### Scilla sibirica*** *Uses* Window-box.

An easy spring-flowering bulb, the small blue flowers are best appreciated at close quarters which is why a window-box is more suitable than a trough or tub.

**Tulips, early double\*\*\*** *Uses* Tub; trough; window-box.

Tall-growing large-flowered tulips are best avoided – they suffer too much in the wind. Double tulips have a dwarf habit and strong stems, and the fuller flowers mean that they do not suffer so much from the wind.

**Tulipa, species and hybrids\*\*\*** *Uses* Growing bag; tub; trough; window-box.

The tulip species, and some of their hybrids, are especially useful because they are dwarf in habit but often large in flower. They also tend to flower early and are generally easier to appreciate in containers than at ground level. There are lots of varieties from which to choose. You should find plenty among the hybrids of *T. fosteriana*, *T. greigii* and *T. kaufmanniana*.

---

## BEDDING PLANTS

This is a rather loosely-termed group of plants, convenient to cover some as diverse as hardy annuals (such as sweet alyssum) and tender perennials (the popular 'geranium'). The common link is that they are suitable for planting out in late spring or early summer, will put on a good display for a season, then either die or have to be taken into the greenhouse or indoors for the winter.

It is not a good idea to sow hardy annuals (plants that can be sown outdoors where they are to flower the same year) directly into a window-box or trough. The box will look extremely untidy for a month or two, and trying to arrange a good display from *in situ* sowing usually leads to disappointment. It is better to raise the plant in boxes or pots and to set out the young plants.

The type of plant (half-hardy annual, tender perennial, etc) is shown at the end of each entry.

Whatever kind of container you are planting, it is usually worth trying to incorporate a few foliage plants, unless of course you are dealing with single-subject planting.

**Ageratum\*\*\*** *Uses* Hanging basket; trough; window-box.

Avoid the less-common tall varieties, and the white-flowered ones which can look tatty as they pass their best. Half-hardy annual.

**Alyssum maritimum (Lobularia maritima) (sweet alyssum, white alyssum)\*\*\*** *Uses* Hanging basket; trough; tubs; window-box.

Alyssums can be coarse and straggly or delicate and compact. Keep to the latter varieties, such as 'Carpet of Snow' and 'Snowdrift' or 'Snow Carpet'. A useful edging plant for containers. Perhaps too despised because of its common association with blue lobelia, but try it on its own, or in a hanging basket dotted among the other plants. Hardy annual.

**Begonia semperflorens (fibrous-rooted begonia)\*\*** *Uses* Growing bag; hanging basket; trough; window-box.

*Begonia semperflorens* – a mass of flower the whole summer.

These are among the very best container plants and will flower all summer; with the various flower colours, and bronze as well as green leaves. By choosing different varieties quite stunning results can be achieved. They are not easy to raise from seed yourself, but plants are widely available in late spring. Half-hardy annual.

### Begonia, tuberous-rooted★ *Uses*
Trough; window-box.

The large-flowered tuberous-rooted begonias sold as dried tubers *can* make good container plants, but are usually best in a favourable summer and warm areas. In a wet season the flowers look a sorry sight and are prone to rot.

If you plant dry tubers you will be disappointed. They must be started off indoors and planted out in growth. Some seed-raised plants may be available and these should be suitable. There is no need to pay a lot for plants for outdoors: seed-raised varieties such as 'Nonstop' and 'Clips' are perfectly good for window-box or trough displays, though they have more impact as single-subject plantings.

For hanging baskets you can buy pendulous varieties. They are generally most effective in a basket of their own, several to one basket. Tender perennial.

### Bellis perennis (double daisy)★★★
*Uses* Trough; window-box.

These are neat spring-flowering plants that have a compactness that makes them useful container plants. There are many

106

Pendulous begonias – at their best with several in one basket.

Tuberous-rooted begonias – some of the modern varieties are perfectly suitable for summer bedding and for growing in containers.

varieties, ranging from small, tight pompon-like flowers to the large more open double flowers. Well worth growing, alone or in association with spring-flowering bulbs or other biennials. Hardy biennial.

### Cheiranthus cheiri (wallflower)★★
*Uses* Trough; window-box.

Although wallflowers are commonplace spring-flowering plants, they are often disappointing in containers. Tall, sparse, and rather leggy plants may still be fragrant but they are a poor substitute for well-grown plants. Choose a *dwarf* variety, start with good, stocky plants, and pinch out the growing points in early autumn to encourage bushiness. Get

them planted in good time, and the results should be pleasing. Hardy biennial.

### Cineraria maritima 'Diamond'★★★
*Uses* Tub; trough; window-box.

This variety has divided leaves with white, woolly hairs and is a useful contrast to most other bedding plants. Although now called *Senecio bicolor* you will almost certainly find it sold as cineraria. There are other varieties, some with more finely divided leaves. Although hardy in some areas, they really have to be overwintered in a greenhouse. Mostly, they are propagated from seed each spring, being treated as half-hardy annuals.

A single fuchsia in a large pot will provide a spectacular and long-lasting display, but you need to be able to overwinter the plant to get a show like this.

**Fuchsia★★** *Uses* Hanging basket; tub; trough; window-box.

Fuchsias are among the most impressive container plants. Although seen at their very best in single-subject baskets or grown as standards in large pots, they will contribute much to a mixed planting too. It is important to choose varieties with the right habit. Do not assume that the hardiest species are the best for growing outdoors in summer; they are too large for containers, although 'Tom Thumb', which is often grown outdoors, is very suitable. Generally, though, it is the large-flowered type that is used, but you will need to choose those recommended for the garden (specialist catalogues will give you this information), and for baskets and often for window-boxes it is the cascading type that you need. Among the basket varieties to look for are 'Cascade', 'Golden Marinka', 'Mantilla', 'Marinka', 'Pink Galore', 'Red Spider', 'Swingtime', and 'Texas Longhorn'. If you angle the root-ball when planting, you will encourage the cascading effect from an early stage. A large basket with an upright fuchsia in the centre and three cascading ones round the edge (stick to one variety for these) can look very impressive. Or miss out the one in the centre and insert an empty pot to make watering easier.

Be sure to feed fuchsias regularly. Avoid a very windy position, and make sure the plants do not dry out. Tender perennial.

**Helichrysum petiolatum\*\*** *Uses*
Hanging basket; tub; window-box.

This is a grey-leaved, rather woolly plant with stiff, arching or cascading stems. A popular hanging basket plant among professionals but not much used by amateurs. You will need to overwinter it in a frost-free place, and may have to shop around for plants. A very worthwhile plant to include if you can find it, however. Tender perennial.

**Impatiens (busy Lizzie)\*\*\*** *Uses*
Growing bag; hanging basket; trough; window-box.

If you buy the plants (you need a heated greenhouse to raise them from seed), the modern strains of impatiens are fantastic container plants. They flower all summer, are easy to grow, and will grow in sun or shade. In fact they are one of the best plants for containers in a shady position.

The variety is important, because some

*Fuchsia* 'Cascade', a variety with a good pendulous habit.

are much more compact than others (and you do not want the indoor type such as the New Guinea hybrids). For hanging baskets some of the most useful are 'Supernova' series and the 'Novette' series. For other containers taller-growing types may be suitable. For a trough the double-flowered varieties can make pretty and interesting plants. Half-hardy annual/tender perennial.

Beneath this mound of impatiens is a large strawberry pot, long since submerged beneath the mass of foliage and flowers.

### Kochia (burning bush)*** *Uses* Tub.

This is a useful foliage plant, though rather large for most window-boxes. It has a green, feathery appearance during the summer, turning purplish-red in late autumn, and needs to be used as a centrepiece for other plants. Half-hardy annual.

### Lobelia** *Uses* Hanging basket; trough; window-box.

This needs no introduction. The trailing varieties are much used in the front of window-boxes and in hanging baskets. Try putting the ordinary compact varieties in the sides of a hanging basket; they can look as effective as the trailing sort. Lobelia is not as foolproof as many gardeners assume. If a basket is neglected, especially if watering

suffers, the lobelia will be one of the first plants to shrivel and give up growing. Watered well and fed, however, it can be magnificent. Half-hardy annual.

### Marigold, African (Tagetes erecta)*** *Uses* Tub; trough; window-box.

The older, tall varieties of African marigolds are not good container plants, but the smaller, compact type (which have sacrificed little in size of flower) like the Space Age series, such as 'Moonshot' and 'Apollo', and the Inca series, are well worth a place. Only plant them if you are prepared to remove the unsightly dead flower heads. Half-hardy annual.

### Marigold, French (Tagetes patula)*** *Uses* Tub, trough; window-box.

These magnificent container plants will flower all summer, and are one of the most foolproof. They are perhaps taken for granted because of their familiarity, but are not to be overlooked. The only problem comes with choosing the varieties, as there are so many of them. Be guided by size and habit as much as colour. Bear in mind that some of the Afro-French type can make quite large, bushy plants. Half-hardy annual.

### Myosotis (forget-me-not)*** *Uses* Tub.

Widely planted, especially interplanted with spring-flowering bulbs, they can however be too rampant in growth for many containers. In tubs, though, they

Impatiens in a recycled cellulose fibre trough.

seem far more at home, especially with other spring-flowering plants. They will self-seed very freely, so can become a nuisance if the seed-heads are not removed before the seeds are scattered. Hardy biennial.

### Nemesia strumosa* *Uses* Trough; window-box.

Most people would probably regard this as a very easy plant, perhaps because it is so widely grown. Unfortunately it is not easy to grow well; a quite modest check will bring the display to an abrupt end, and even at their best they are short-lived in comparison with many other bedding plants. Start with good, sturdy plants that have not received a check to growth, and keep well watered, and fed regularly. Then they can be rewarding. Half-hardy annual.

### Nicotiana alata (tobacco plant)★★★
*Uses* Growing bag; tub; trough.

These are first-class container plants where a tall, upright plant is needed. Some of the modern varieties, such as the Domino series, are small and compact (about 30 cm/1 ft), with upward-facing flowers, but they still do not have the right habit for a good window-box plant. In troughs and tubs, however, they are both pretty and fragrant. Make sure that you buy a day-opening variety (such as 'Nicki' or 'Domino'). Some of the taller varieties can be suitable for a large tub in the right setting. Half-hardy annual.

### Pansy (Viola × wittrockiana)★★ *Uses* Trough; window-box.

Among the mass of other summer-flowering plants they can become lost in a container of mixed plants, but are a good choice for a small, perhaps old-fashioned trough as a single-subject planting. Winter-flowering pansies (even if they flower in early spring) are also invaluable, and usually more appreciated. Pansies respond to dead-heading. Hardy biennial/half-hardy annual.

### Pelargonium zonale (geranium)★★★
*Uses* Tub; trough; window-box; hanging basket.

It is hard to imagine gardens without these useful plants. They tolerate the sometimes dry conditions in containers very well, and will flower for months. There are so many varieties now, many of them seed-raised, that the choice is bewildering. There are general principles, however, that it is worth following.

The trailing ivy-leaved 'geraniums' (actually these are *P. peltatum*) are at the time of writing propagated vegetatively, and you will almost certainly buy pot-grown named varieties, most of which will do well in baskets or window-boxes. There are, however, seed raised ivy-leaved in the pipeline, although for containers that really matter it is likely that the traditional varieties will remain the best.

An old chimney-pot put to good use as a home for geraniums.

The many seed-raised zonal pelargoniums ('geraniums') are superb for bedding, but for containers there is still a lot to be said for sticking to traditional varieties. If you start with large, healthy plants these take some beating. Half-hardy annual/tender perennial.

**Petunia\*\*** *Uses* Growing bag; hanging basket; tub; trough; window-box.

Another traditional container plant, but interestingly one about which experts often disagree. Some dismiss them as undesirable hanging basket plants, for instance, whereas others think that no hanging basket is complete without them. It is not difficult to grow them well, but variety *is* important. Choose a

Petunias in a terracotta pot − a simple but effective combination.

Petunias in a growing bag on a balcony.

compact variety that resists wet weather. The Resisto range is very good, and 'Resisto Rose' an outstanding plant. A poor summer will sort out the good from the bad. In tubs, petunias are often most effective on their own. Half-hardy annual.

**Primula polyantha (polyanthus)***
*Uses* Tub; trough.

Very useful spring-flowering plants anywhere in the garden, and they can make a good display in troughs and tubs either on their own or in association with other spring-flowering plants. Hardy perennial (treated as hardy biennial).

**Primula vulgaris (P. acaulis) (primrose)*** *Uses* Trough; window-box.

The modern primroses are far removed from the wild primrose. You can raise your own from seed, but it is probably easier to buy plants when they are on sale from late winter and plunge the pot in a window-box.

**Rudbeckia (black-eyed Susan, cone flower)*** *Uses* Tub.

These plants are best as a single-subject planting in a good-sized container. They will make an absolutely stunning show. Choose a dwarf variety such as 'Marmalade' (single) or 'Goldilocks' (double and semi-double). Half-hardy annual.

**Salvia*** *Uses* Trough; tub; window-box.

Salvias are popular bedding plants, but not so widely used in containers. This is a pity, because they are bright (at least the red varieties) and long-lasting. If the growing tips are pinched out while the plants are young they will be bushy too. They are well worth considering, either as a single-subject planting or mixed with other bedding plants. Half-hardy annual.

Modern hybrid primroses, in a shallow asbestos-cement container raised on screen walling blocks.

**Tropaeolum majus (nasturtium)\*\*\***
*Uses* Window-box; hanging basket.

Trailing nasturtiums are best forgotten, but there are compact varieties that can make a brilliant contribution to the summer colour if you are prepared to combat the almost inevitable blackfly that they seem to attract from miles around. For window-boxes the 'Gleam Hybrids' are popular, but for hanging baskets these have to some extent been ousted by 'Whirlybird', which has semi-double upward-facing flowers held well above the foliage. Hardy annual.

**Verbena\*\*** *Uses* Hanging basket; trough; tub.

Improved varieties seem to have made verbena a more popular plant. Single plants tend to get lost among the other plants, but they make a bright massed display. Half-hardy annual.

Nasturtium 'Gleam Hybrids'. One of the best varieties for containers.

Shrubs may not be among the most spectacular container plants, but they are among the most useful. Even if you change seasonal plants two or three times a year, there will still be 'in between times' with little of interest. Of course herbaceous plants and bulbs have the same shortcoming. Shrubs, on the other hand, have a much longer season of interest, and evergreens will make a contribution the year round.

The list of shrubs below ranges from dwarfs for a window-box to those that will need quite a large shrub tub. Nearly all of them will outgrow the container in due course, but not for many seasons in most cases; and then they can be planted in the ground so that you have a growing investment.

This list is confined to just over 20 because of space limitations. It could be four times that length and still exclude some useful plants, but the shortlist will give an idea of the diverse types of shrubs that can be used.

### Agave americana 'Marginata' ('Variegata')* *Uses* Tub. *Merits* Evergreen; foliage.

It seems odd to start a shrub list with a plant that is not really a shrub, but it happens to be the most convenient place for this Mexican succulent! It really is a most striking container plant, looking especially good in a terracotta pot, with its bold variegated spiky leaves. Its only drawback is that it is not really a frost-hardy plant, although there are large specimens that are left outdoor exposed to frost and come to no harm. It is a gamble, but one that you might like to take if you live in say a coastal area that does not receive severe frosts, but elsewhere you may think it worth moving the container to a more protected environment for the winter.

### Aucuba japonica (spotted laurel)*** *Uses* Tub; trough; window-box. *Merits* Evergreen; foliage.

In complete contrast to the agave, this is as tough as they come, and will even thrive in shade. Choose one of the attractively-variegated varieties such as 'Crotonifolia'.

### Buxus sempervirens (box)*** *Uses* Tub. *Merits* Evergreen; foliage.

Many people regard the box as a rather dull plant, but there are variegated forms such as 'Aureovariegata' (yellow variegation) and 'Elegantissima' (creamy-white variegation). For a small container, consider the dwarf edging box, *B. s.* 'Suffruticosa'.

### Camellia** *Uses* Tub. *Merits* Evergreen; flowers.

Provided you use an acid compost, camellias will make rewarding tub plants. The glossy evergreen leaves are always handsome, and the flowers in spring can be spectacular. There are many kinds, but you should be pleased with any of the *C. japonica* varieties, such as 'Adolphe

Audusson', and *C.* × *williamsii* hybrids such as 'Donation'.

**Chamaerops humilis*** *Uses* Tub. *Merits* Evergreen; foliage.

This is a dwarf palm that rarely exceeds 1.5 m (5 ft), and is hardy in mild areas. Being a small palm, it is easy enough to take indoors for the worst months anyway. It is useful where you need a touch of distinction.

**Cordyline australis (cabbage tree, Torbay palm)*** *Uses* Tub. *Merits* Evergreen; foliage.

This palm-like plant is hardy in mild areas, but not suitable for leaving outdoors where there are normally prolonged and severe frosts. It can look out of place in a small garden and needs a suitable setting.

**Euonymus fortunei\*\*\*** *Uses* Tub; trough; window-box. *Merits* Evergreen; foliage.

There are two varieties that are particularly useful for containers: 'Emerald Gaiety' (white variegation) and 'Emerald 'n' Gold' (green, gold, and pink-tinged leaves). They are useful carpeters to put between other shrubs.

**Fatsia japonica\*\*\*** *Uses* Tub; trough; window-box. *Merits* Evergreen; foliage.

This is one of the very best tub shrubs. The hand-like large green leaves on a plant that always looks elegant are a year-round attraction. The white, ball-shaped flower heads in autumn provide an interesting bonus on established plants. Small plants can be started off in troughs or window-boxes, and moved on to tubs later.

**Hebe × franciscana 'Variegata'\*\*\*** *Uses* Tub; trough; window-box. *Merits* Evergreen; foliage.

Neat, compact, evergreen, bright variegation, perhaps a bonus of blue flowers − what more could one ask?

**Hebe pinguifolia 'Pagei'\*\*\*** *Uses* Trough, window-box. *Merits* Evergreen; foliage; flowers.

It may soon outgrow its space, having a naturally low, spreading habit, but will make a very useful garden plant afterwards. It has silver-grey leaves, and a mass of small white flowers in late spring.

**Hedera (ivy)\*\*\*** *Uses* Hanging basket; tub; trough; window-box. *Merits* Evergreen; foliage.

Ivy needs no introduction but keep to small-leaved forms of *H. helix*. There are many varieties with attractively variegated foliage. Ivy does best trailing over the edge of a container.

**Laurus nobilis (sweet bay)*** *Uses* Tub. *Merits* Evergreen; foliage.

It is popular as a clipped specimen. Grown as an ordinary shrub, there are more interesting plants, but clipped into an oval outline, or as a ball on a 'trunk', they become highly desirable plants. In areas subject to long, severe frosts they

*Fatsia japonica*, one of the best shrubs for a large container where you want a bold, dramatic outline.

will need protection, but should be safe outdoors in favourable districts.

**Mahonia 'Charity'\*\*\*** *Uses* Tub. *Merits* Evergreen; foliage; flowers.

This shrub is useful not only because of its large leaves but also because it bears its fragrant flowers in late autumn and early winter.

**Nerium oleander (oleander)\*** *Uses* Tub. *Merits* Evergreen; flowers.

This Mediterranean plant makes a good tub shrub for the patio in summer,

*Hebe × franciscana* 'Variegata' in a white plastic container.

but it needs the protection of a conservatory or cool greenhouse in winter.

### Phormium tenax (New Zealand flax)** Uses Tub. *Merits* Evergreen; foliage.

The sword-like leaves make phormiums very striking tub plants, especially if you choose varieties with coloured and variegated foliage. Heights vary considerably, so be careful to choose a variety that will be suitable for the size of container and the setting. They will need protection in very cold areas, but are not harmed by moderate frosts.

### Prunus lusitanica (Portugal laurel)*** Uses Tub. *Merits* Evergreen; foliage.

Sometimes dismissed as a rather coarse hedging plant, but it can be clipped to make a small-headed standard tree that will be cheaper than using sweet bay.

### Rhododendron** Uses Tub. *Merits* Evergreen; flowers.

Rhododendrons are magnificent flowering shrubs, and if you garden on alkaline soil growing them in tubs will enable you to give them the acid compost that they require.

Think carefully about variety. Most large-flowered types can be grown in containers for several years, but it is a pity if they outgrow the space just as they are producing a worthwhile amount of flower. The *R. yakushimanum* hybrids are worth searching out.

### Senecio monroi*** Uses Tub; trough; window-box. *Merits* Evergreen; foliage; flowers.

Grey-leaved with yellow flowers in mid-summer, this small plant can be used in a window-box or trough, and moved to a tub when it becomes too large.

### Trachycarpus fortunei (Chusan palm)* Uses Tub. *Merits* Evergreen; foliage.

This fairly tough palm will withstand a lot of frost, but still needs protection in cold areas.

### Yucca filamentosa*** Uses Tub. *Merits* Evergreen; foliage; flowers.

This plant never fails to catch the attention when in flower, and is striking even out of flower. It is hardier than it looks, and should survive in all but the coldest parts.

## HERBACEOUS PLANTS

Herbaceous plants (those that live from year to year but die down during the winter) are not ideal container plants. Unless you turn them out each autumn and replant the following spring, there is no opportunity to use the container for another group of plants for the winter. It is worth considering them, however, if you want to add a bit of variety to the more usual run-of-the-mill container

Hostas are good for livening up otherwise dull corners.

plants. The list of plants below is by no means exhaustive, but is intended to reflect the type of herbaceous plant that could be used. The plants chosen should have interesting foliage over a long season, rather than a short display of brilliant flower but little other merit.

**Bergenia\*\*\*** *Uses* Trough, window-box. *Merits* Evergreen; foliage; flowers.

The leaves actually persist through the winter, usually taking on purplish or reddish tinges, so this is a particularly useful plant. It is tough, and shade-tolerant. It is really best as a single-subject planting.

**Carex morowii\*\*\*** *Uses* Trough; window-box. *Merits* Evergreen; foliage.

This ornamental grass-like sedge is a useful filler among other plants.

**Festuca ovina 'Glauca'\*\*\*** *Uses* Trough; window-box. *Merits* Evergreen; foliage.

This is a grass with blue-grey foliage that acts as a useful foil for other plants in a mixed container.

**Hosta\*\*** *Uses* Tub; trough. *Merits* Foliage.

This is an unlikely candidate because hostas prefer moist conditions, something not associated with containers. If you keep them in a reasonably shady place, however, and well watered, the variegated kinds can make really striking container plants.

## SOME USEFUL CONIFERS

Dwarf conifers are something that you usually love or hate. Whatever your instinctive feelings about them, some make very useful container plants. Not all tolerate dry roots, however, so size alone is not the only consideration. Go round any garden centre and you will see just how many dwarf conifers are available; the selection below is a mere starting point, although it is probably best not to overdo the number that you use.

*Chamaecyparis lawsoniana* 'Ellwoodii'.
*C. obtusa* 'Nana'.
*C. pisifera* 'Boulevard'.
*C. p.* 'Nana'.
*Cryptomeria japonica* 'Elegans Compacta'.

Dwarf conifers, *Euonymus fortunei* 'Emerald Gaiety' and small-leaved ivies in a plastic trough.

*Juniperis communis* 'Compressa'.
*Juniperis communis* 'Hibernica'.
*Juniperis communis* 'Repanda'.
*Juniperis horizontalis*.
*Thuja occidentalis* 'Rheingold'.

## TREES

Trees are not 'naturals' for containers, but sometimes a situation calls for a small tree in a (large) container. Local authorities sometime manage to grow a whole range of quite large trees in containers, but these are often much larger than would be appropriate in a normal garden. It makes good sense to confine your tree-growing efforts to specimens of modest proportions. Choose shrubby types of trees, such as *Magnolia stellata* or *M.* × *loebneri*. Even such fast-growers as the stag's-horn sumach *(Rhus typhina)* can be contained satisfactorily for quite a few years. Some of the Japanese maples (*Acer palmatum* varieties) make pretty container trees and are generally slow-growing in tubs. They need protection from strong or cold spring winds, but are otherwise easy.

## PLANTS FOR SINK GARDENS AND TROUGHS

Sink gardens and troughs need small, but not invasive, plants. That encompasses many hundreds of alpines, of which those below are just a representative sample. It does not include very dwarf conifers and shrubs that are also useful.

*Achillea* 'King Edward'.
*Aethionema* 'Warley Rose'.
*Androsace chumbyi*.
*Arabis ferdinandi-coburgi* 'Variegata'.
*Armeria caespitosa (A. juniperifolia)*.
*Armeria maritima*.
*Campanula carpatica*.
*Campanula cochleariifolia*.
*Cyclamen hederifolium*.
*Dianthus alpinus*.
*Gentiana acaulis*.
*Gentiana verna*.
*Geranium cinereum subcaulescens*.
*Hepatica nobilis (H. triloba)*.
*Hypericum olypicum*.
*Lewisia* 'Rose Splendour'.
*Leontopodium alpinum*.
*Primula farinosa*.
*Phlox douglasii*.
*Rhodohypoxis baurii*.
*Raoulia australis*.
*Saxifraga oppositifolia*.
*Saxifraga paniculata (S. aizoon)* 'Rosea'
*Saxifraga cochlearis minor* (and many other saxifrages).
*Sedum cauticolum*.
*Sedum lydium*.
*Sedum spathulifolium*.
*Sempervivum tectorum* (and many other sempervivums).
*Silene alpestris*.
*Soldanella alpina*.

# 9·HERBS AND VEGETABLES

This is the smallest chapter in the book. That is because vegetables in troughs and window-boxes make neither a serious contribution to the kitchen nor an attractive addition to the garden. For those gardeners who find it fun to grow a few vegetables this way such pro-

A healthy crop of lettuces in a growing bag.

nouncements must seem heresy. The defence is that vegetable growing in containers can be fun, and satisfying if you do not expect too much. If you really want vegetables that will contribute to the family budget, however, then this is not the way to go about growing them. Having said that, you can expect some successes, especially if you use growing

bags. This brief chapter will suggest only those vegetables that are easy and worthwhile in containers.

**Carrots** are good in growing bags and even in window-boxes, *provided you choose a round or stump-rooted forcing variety.*

**French beans** are worth a try in a growing bag.

**Lettuce** is one of the most dependable. Use a growing bag.

**Marrow and courgettes** are possibles for growing bags, but you need lots of room.

**Radishes** are easy, in growing bags or troughs or boxes.

**Runner beans** can be successful in growing bags, and are quite ornamental. You need to solve the support problem.

**Tomatoes** are fine for growing bags. It is best to go for a bush variety such as

Ordinary varieties of tomato are unsuitable for growing in pots outside, but there are suitable varieties if you are prepared for a relatively small crop. This is 'Florida Petite'.

Herb window-boxes can be pretty as well as useful.

'Red Alert' outdoors. You can try the mini-tomatoes such as 'Minibel' and 'Tiny Tim' in window-boxes and hanging baskets. The crop will be small, the flavour probably not impressive. They are, however, fun to grow.

**Herbs** can make an attractive as well as a useful contribution to the garden, and suitable ones will enhance a special herb pot or even a window-box. Among the most suitable for these containers are chives, sweet marjoram, parsley, and various thymes.